14 95

MONTANA'S
Continental Divide

NUMBER TWELVE

MONTANA GEOGRAPHIC SERIES

BY BILL CUNNINGHAM

D1305731

PUBLISHED BY

Montana Magazine, Inc.

HELENA, MONTANA 59604

RICK GRAETZ, PUBLISHER
MARK THOMPSON, DIRECTOR OF PUBLICATIONS
BARBARA FIFER, ASSISTANT BOOK EDITOR
CAROLYN CUNNINGHAM, EDITOR—MONTANA MAGAZINE

This series intends to fill the need for in-depth information about Montana subjects. The geographic concept explores the historical color, the huge landscape and the resilient people of a single Montana subject area. Design by Len Visual Design, Helena, Montana. All camera prep work and layout production completed in Helena, Montana. Typesetting by Thurber Printing, Helena, Montana. Printed in Japan by DNP America, San Francisco.

Dedication

This book is dedicated to my parents, who helped instill in me a love for those things wild, free and geographical.

The Author

Bill Cunningham, a fourth-generation Montanan now living Missoula, is a forester who once taught at the University of Montana School of Forestry. After working a decade for wilderness conservation groups in Montana, he is now active in wildland teaching, writing and outfitting.

Montana Magazine, Inc.
Box 5630
Helena, Montana 59604
ISBN 0-938314-23-8

©1986 Montana Magazine, Inc.

Acknowledgements

My role as author of this book has been that of compiler. I think of the countless hours of gathering, sorting, discarding, digesting and recycling vast amounts of information, filtered through the reservoir of my own knowledge, experience and personal philosophy so as to produce a starting point. This modest beginning would not have been publishable were it not for the unselfish help, encouragement and critical review of many people. The remaining errors and omissions are my sole responsibility.

I first want to acknowledge the superb and always cheerful assistance of Jud Moore, the Forest Service Information Officer for Region One. Other Forest Service folks who were helpful include Janet Johnson, Gary Fairchild and Tina Schwartzman. I am particularly grateful to Dr. Stephen Arno, Forest Ecologist with the U.S. Forest Service. Steve's excellent new book, *Timberline,* was an indispensible reference for Continental Divide vegetation.

When I began this project I dreaded the laborious search that would be needed for the history chapter. My dread was short-lived thanks to the invaluable help of Dave Walter and Ellie Arguimbau of the Montana Historical Society. Lory Morrow, photo archivist for the Society, was also of great assistance. Vital historical and archival materials also were provided by the following: Beth Ladeau of the George C. Ruhle Library at Glacier National Park; Ellen Seeley, photo archivist for Glacier National Park; Dale Johnson of the University of Montana Mansfield Library Archives, and Tom Kotynski and Marge Foote of the *Great Falls Tribune*.

Many highly professional people took time from their busy lives to give information and provide technical review of the painfully crude drafts that were thrust upon them. I especially want to thank Dr. John Craighead and Roland Redmond of the Wildlife-Wildlands Institute, Gayle Joslin, Rich DeSimone, and Jim Posewitz of the Montana Department of Fish, Wildlife and Parks, Dr. Robert Ream and Ken Wall of the University of Montana Wilderness Institute, and Bob Cooney. Bob especially helped remove the pain from seemingly endless research with his wonderful tales of early days along the Continental Divide in the Bob Marshall country.

A special note of gratitude is due James R. Wolf, Executive Director of the Continental Divide Trail Society. Jim generously allowed me to adapt my text on the proposed Continental Divide National Scenic Trail from his excellent set of Guide Books. His careful review of the text, as with the others listed above, added immensely to the accuracy and readability of the following pages.

I would be remiss if I failed to mention the cooperation of those citizens of the Great Divide whose activities are profiled in this book. For their patience in enduring my probing camera and questions, I want to thank Augusta outfitters Max and Ann Barker, Big Hole ranchers Jack Hirschy and J.B. Anderson, Big Hole pioneer Leo Hagel, and Helena-area ranchers Chase and Scott Hibbard.

I am indebted to *Montana Magazine* publisher Rick Graetz for inspiring me to write the book, and for periodically reminding me that I was once again behind in my work schedule. My good friend Al Luebeck of Butte also helped in ways that he may not fully realize. Al's companionship on a number of southwest Montana Continental Divide photo tours took the work out of these excursions.

Each of these people, and others to whom I apologize for not listing, made this book possible. But there is one who stands out above all others, my friend Ellie Arguimbau. Ellie got me going on the initial research in her capacity as an archivist for the Montana Historical Society. More importantly, her ability to help me overcome procrastination resulted in the completion of this book.

Preface

When I first set out to write a book about Montana's Continental Divide I knew that I would have to overcome my natural tendency to write only about peaks, mountains and wilderness. This tendency is almost ingrained from a love affair with Montana wild country that seems to grow with each passing year. Fortunately, through researching and writing this book I have learned that the Continental Divide is indeed mountains and wilderness, but that it is so much more.

As you read through the chapters dealing with such non-wilderness topics as history, roads, railways, place names and lifestyles, please consider the greater significance of Montana's dividing ridge.

Much of the Continental Divide in the state remains as early white explorers first encountered it, a wild and free remnant of a vanishing past. But the Divide is also people. Indeed, much of the drama and excitement of the only unbroken ridge across the depth of Montana stems from those varied uses that we have made of it.

These uses go to the very core of the American Dream, the idea that we can overcome the once insurmountable barrier of the Rockies. Explorers, trappers, surveyors, road-builders, railroaders, miners, loggers, land promoters, and tourists each saw the high crest in a different way for different purposes. Their common desire to extract wealth and passage from the Great Divide has melded into a history rich with humor, tragedy, exploitation and stewardship. You will find some of this richness displayed in the following pages.

The process of learning more about Montana's most important geographical/topographical feature has had a humbling effect, because I know how much more there is to learn. I hope that you enjoy exploring the Great Divide, as presented in this book, as much as I have in writing about it.

MONTANA'S
Continental Divide

Contents

Opposite page, left to right: *The Continental Divide southeast of Eighteenmile Peak.* BILL CUNNINGHAM
Lima Peaks and east fork, Little Sheep Creek. GEORGE WUERTHNER
Sunset on the Divide, by Badger Pass. GEORGE WUERTHNER
Hoary marmot. MARK WALLNER
This page, left to right: MICHAEL FRANCIS
Autumn on MacDonald Pass. MIKE LOGAN
Logan Pass, Glacier National Park. GEORGE WUERTHNER
Early-morning view of Little Lake on the Divide in the west Big Hole. BILL CUNNINGHAM

Introduction

For purposes of introducing the special qualities of Montana's high crest I concluded that two points above all others were the most relevant: the point at which the Continental Divide enters Montana from the north, and the point at which it leaves the state to the south. Significantly, these two locations share the distinction of being in two of America's oldest, largest and most magnificent national parks, Glacier and Yellowstone. They are both remote and inaccessible. Therein the similarity ends, as you will discover as you join me on three trips to the different worlds of the Divide's most widely-separated points in Montana.

The Continental Divide at the 49th Parallel

The weather report called for heavy snows at the 6,000' level in Glacier Park. Fine, Glacier is indeed heavy snow country, but on August 15? Still, I was determined to make the tough hike to the northern geographic beginning of Montana's Continental Divide: the exact point where the Divide enters the United States at the 49th Parallel. It is also where the Canadian Provinces of Alberta and British Columbia meet Montana on the northern boundary of Glacier Park. Thus, in many ways survey point #272 had symbolic as well as physical significance to the subject of this Geographic. *It was a place I had to reach.*

A study of the topographic map revealed that the best route would be from Alberta's Waterton Park. About one mile north of Cameron Lake is a mile-long trail that climbs some 300 feet to Akamina Pass (5,900') on the Continental Divide. It then appeared that a 2,000' vertical climb two miles south along the Divide to 7,922' Forum Peak would put me near the junction between the Divide and the 49th Parallel. Getting to the actual junction would require a steep, 600' drop from Forum Peak to a high saddle due west of the head of Cameron Lake.

It rained and snowed hard all night and the sky held heavy, dark clouds the next morning. My friend Ellie and I wore rain gear for protection against the wet brush as we climbed along the Divide south of Akamina Pass to the 6,500' snowline. Huckleberries were abundant. We soon

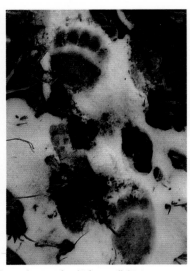

Above, left: *The northernmost point along Montana's Great Divide, where the international boundary at the 49th parallel joins Montana with the Canadian provinces of British Columbia and Alberta. The view here is to southeast toward Glacier National Park.* BILL CUNNINGHAM
Right: *Fresh grizzly tracks atop the Continental Divide add to the feeling of wildness where the Divide meets the 49th parallel.* BILL CUNNINGHAM
Opposite page: *Nowhere is Montana's Divide more impressive than where it forms the Garden Wall in Glacier Park.* BRUCE SELYEM

discovered that we were not the only ones enjoying the sweet wild fruit. Precisely on top of the Divide was a steaming pile of grizzly bear scat.

Before long we came across the tracks of what appeared to be a sow and cub. They had been working the Divide toward us and were likely alerted to our presence as we bushwhacked up the ridge. The eerie mist rising above us, along with the fresh grizzly sign, gave our Continental Divide trek an added feeling of adventure.

It stayed quite cold as we trudged through four inches of wet snow to the abrupt north ridge of Forum Peak. I tried a free climb on a slick sedimentary rock wall only to lose almost all feeling in my hands from the icy cliff. I carefully backed down the rock face, realizing that what was a reasonable route in dry weather was suicidal when wet. Less than a half mile from the 49th Parallel, and faced with sheer cliffs on all sides except the way we had come, we were discouraged but not defeated.

With the imposing peaks to the south poking through the lifting clouds, we decided to head north again along the Divide, drop into the Forum Lake basin, and scramble up a steeper but less technical ridge to the west. The ridge connected to a tundra plateau leading to Forum Peak. By the time we crossed the basin the day was turning beautiful,

with bright sun and dramatic clouds. We struggled to the top of the far saddle on what I've concluded is the slickest substance in the world: beargrass covered with wet snow. Our ascent of the rocky ridge turned out to be more challenging than anticipated, with considerable rock and ledge work.

Once atop the Forum Peak plateau we were awed by the seemingly limitless mountain skyline in all directions. Again, the steep descent along the Divide north of Forum Peak to the 49th Parallel was tougher going than I imagined it would be. Constant route-seeking and detours were necessary. Just as I reached the long-sought international border on the rugged spine of the continent, I was treated to the sight of a bighorn ewe and lamb. Uncertain weather and terrain had made it a tough seven-hour trip, but at last I stood at the historic destination sought by the original boundary survey parties 125 years previously. The 49th Parallel crosses the Continental Divide here on a relatively low bench above an unnamed pass at about 7,400', with spectacular views into the headwaters of two oceans — Montana's Kintla Creek on the Pacific side and Cameron Creek in Alberta on the Hudson Bay side. The untamed beauty of this remote stretch of the Divide is truly a fitting beginning to Montana's Great Divide.

The Continental Divide at the Convergence of Montana, Idaho and Wyoming

The three states of Montana, Idaho and Wyoming touch some two to three miles inside the western boundary of Yellowstone Park. To reach this significant but little-known spot, I drove for miles on a logging highway called the Black Canyon loop road to the 8,000'-foot-high bench of the Moose Creek Plateau. I reasoned that if I could just find the Continental Divide, which at this point separates Montana's Gallatin National Forest from Idaho's Targhee National Forest, I could proceed southeast to the only place along the entire Great Divide where three states intersect.

Rain, wind and hail greeted me as I set out on a north compass bearing to find the hidden Divide among the flat lodgepole pine forest. Suddenly, I came to a vast logging clearcut amidst a maze of forest roads. Then another clearcut and more roads. How could this be? By my reckoning I was not only on the Continental Divide but on the boundary of Yellowstone Park as well. The massive clearcuts spilled over on both sides of the elusive Divide, obliterating whatever Montana-Idaho boundary markers once existed.

Confused by the endless network of logging roads I found myself wandering in a widening circle on both sides of the Divide. The lateness of the hour forced me to abandon my search for the tri-state Divide point as I reluctantly determined that the refuge of my car was a more attainable objective.

Unwilling to admit defeat, two weeks later I again drove up the Black Canyon road out of Island Park, Idaho. This time, instead of bushwhacking north from the road, Ellie and I decided to hike up Black Canyon itself. Unfortunately, I forgot the actual 15' topographic map for the area. Still, we were confident that we could wind our way up Black Canyon (named for a bed of gleaming obsidian along its course) to within one-half mile west of our goal. Upon reaching the Divide, we would follow it east-southeast to the junction of the three states. Simple.

The only positive thing that I can say about our route is that we did manage to avoid that maze of clearcuts and logging roads by confining our journey almost entirely within Yellowstone Park. But the central problem remained — actually locating the Divide in this flat, heavily timbered plateau country.

Suddenly, I found a Montana-Idaho boundary post indicating that we were not only on the Divide but also east

of the great intersection. More thick brush and blowdown, and then another boundary post. Our hopes soared. Maybe, just maybe we would find the elusive point on what seemed an imaginary Divide. Two frustrating hours later we concluded that despite continual reference to the compass we had been stumbling through the level jungle in a huge circle with no idea where the Divide itself was, let alone the pinpoint on the map that we were seeking. We began to wonder if the Divide was no more than an idea in the mind of a sadistic mapmaker.

There was no choice but to return to our vehicle, which we calculated to be about three miles southwest. Upon studying the Buffalo Lake topo map the next day we learned that we had indeed run circles around the elusive point on the just-as-elusive Divide. When we turned around we were at least a half mile inside Wyoming, east of the three-state confluence. Without question, we were within a few yards of the intersection but the dense forest and undergrowth prevented us from finding the actual monument.

I can't help but reflect on the incredible contrast between the rugged, majestic character of the Great Divide as it enters Montana from the north into Glacier Park, and the flat, subdued, and indefinite nature of this same hydrologic ridge as it leaves Montana to the south in Yellowstone Park. The Continental Divide is a feature of constantly changing moods, contrasts and endless diversity. Nowhere along its 800-mile course in Montana is this contrast more striking than at these two points, in Glacier and in Yellowstone.

The Continental Divide is an astonishing reality. It is in fact a hemispheric Divide, splitting watersheds from Alaska's Brooks Range through the Andes to the Strait of Magellan. Its length of at least 25,000 miles exceeds the circumference of the earth. After focusing much of my energies on the Divide during the past year and a half, I've come to realize that no one person will ever know all of the Continental Divide in Montana, let alone throughout the hemisphere.

The Great Divide has a profound life-shaping influence in Montana, not just because of its physical reality but because it literally divides the state into two distinct regions: the mountainous one third in the west and the high plains and prairies of the eastern two thirds.

It would be difficult to imagine Montana without the Continental Divide. What if Idaho extended east to the Divide, north of Lost Trail Pass, as it did prior to when Montana became a Territory in 1864? Our "east of the Divide/west of the Divide" consciousness is so deeply embedded in our psyche that most Montanans are scarcely aware of it. The Great Barrier divides not only watersheds and weather, but also opinions — about what the land is

good for. Montanans have an instinct for these differences, but few think about them and fewer still articulate the effect of the Divide on their daily lives.

Montanans do indeed tend to categorize that which is east or west of the Divide — the weather, the country, the forests, the people, and the economy. Some of these differences are explored in the following pages as we examine Montana's five "big W's" —Wildlands, Wildlife, Water, Weather, and a Way of Life intimately tied to the land. Nowhere are these "big W's" better exemplified than along the rugged backbone of the Continent as it winds from Glacier to Yellowstone.

We should distinguish at the outset between the geographer's line that separates drainages, and the mountains through which it runs. The Rockies consists of dozens of lesser ranges in Montana alone. These mountain systems are intermittent; in places the upthrust gives way to broad grasslands and even prairie. The Continental Divide weaves through them in seemingly chaotic fashion — twisting, turning, changing direction from one range to another.

The barrier rises in Glacier Park with decisive suddenness. The Divide leaves Glacier at its lowest point,

Marias Pass, beginning its journey through the heart of the Bob Marshall country. It is here that the awesome Chinese Wall truly does justice to the name Continental Divide. From Rogers Pass to the Anaconda-Pintler Range south of Anaconda, the gentle face of the Divide makes it appear as though nature took a well deserved rest after the strain of sculpting the soaring walls and craggy chasms of the northern Continental Divide region. As the Divide rides the lofty crest of the Anaconda, Bitterroot, Centennial and Henry's Lake Ranges, it once again assumes its popular image.

It is difficult to describe the values and qualities of what is defined throughout this book as "Continental Divide Country." When asked to define these qualities, people will mention scenery, fishing, game, wilderness, and history. What it all boils down to is living room, a sort of spatial insulation from other humans that still characterizes much of Montana and the West. To me, Continental Divide country is predominantly wild land, where instead of calling the shots, humans must bend to a world larger and more powerful than themselves.

The Physical Base

Parting the Waters by Blind Luck

by Dave Alt
Professor of Geology,
University of Montana

The Continental Divide wanders aimlessly across the geologic map of western Montana, following a course that nicely samples several geologic provinces while obeying the dictates of none. The way the water runs has more to do with blind luck than with bedrock.

The streams of Montana, both east and west, began to run sometime between 2 and 3 million years ago. That was when the climate changed from the truly desert conditions that had prevailed for many millions of years to something more like what we know today. That was also about when the first of the great ice ages began. Who knows what that coincidence may mean?

During the millions of desert years, about 30 million of them, western Montana had no streams that went much beyond the floor of the nearest broad valley. We speak here of the broad basins such as the Jefferson or Deer Lodge Valley that formed with the Rocky Mountains and reflect the structure of the earth's crust. Nevada is that way today.

Streams in Nevada and other modern deserts flow into the broad floor of one of the big valleys and dry up, leaving their load of sediment on the valley floor. Such regions have no connected network of streams that drain to the oceans. So desert valleys fill with sediment, a little more every time a heavy rain flushes the canyons in the mountains. Those accumulations of valley-fill sediment commonly reach depths of several thousand feet as the mountains slowly drown in their own debris.

We know western Montana was a desert for a long time, because the big valleys all contain depths of desert valley-fill sediment, thousands of feet of mud, sand, and gravel.

These two little lakes fill a pair of basins eroded in solid bedrock in the floor of a glacial cirque. Glacier National Park. BRUCE SELYEM

And we can be sure that no streams connected the valleys of western Montana during those desert years because all the pebbles in those gravels come from local sources. If a connected network of streams had existed, surely they would have imported at least a few pebbles from distant places.

So the desert valleys of western Montana were closed basins where water and sediment from the surrounding mountains collected, and none drained out. When the climate turned wetter some 2 or 3 million years ago, each of those basins filled like a bathtub to form a lake. And the water rose as the rain continued to fall, until the lake level finally reached the lowest point on the basin rim. Then water spilled over the Divide into the next valley, which in turn overflowed, and so on.

Think of how it must have happened.

The lake that once filled the Silver Bow Valley spilled into the Deer Lodge Valley, for example, establishing Silver Bow Creek. Then the lake in the Deer Lodge Valley overflowed west into the one that flooded the Flint Creek Valley to start the Clark Fork River flowing between Garrison and Drummond. And so it went until all the valleys were connected and the eroding streams of water pouring through the valleys finally drained them. So, the main streams of today descended from the overflow channels that connected lakes after the climate changed sometime between 2 and 3 million years ago. But things could so easily have happened differently.

If some low pass had allowed water to spill east out of the Silver Bow Valley before it found an exit to the west, the Continental Divide might now follow the crest of the Flint Creek Range instead of the East Ridge. Where the water happened to flow was entirely a matter of which divide between valleys happened to have the lowest pass, a matter of purest chance that depended hardly at all upon the bedrock.

So whether you live east or west of the Continental Divide depends upon the gambler's luck of where water happened to start spilling out of those undrained basins. That is why we have to keep changing the subject as we follow the rocks from north to south along the Continental Divide.

Blocks of bright red mudstone from the Kintla formation on the ridge overlooking the glacial cirque that holds Hidden Lake. Near Logan Pass in Glacier National Park. GEORGE WUERTHNER

Glacier National Park—The Lewis Overthrust

Between the Canadian border and McDonald Pass west of Helena the Continental Divide crosses two parts of the northern Montana overthrust belt: Glacier Park and the long ridges that corrugate the Sawtooth Range from north to south.

Most of Glacier Park is a single enormous slab, thousands of feet of Precambrian sedimentary rock that moved at least 35 miles east along a surface called the Lewis overthrust fault. That slab stayed in one piece as it moved, and remained nearly flat. The rocks hardly look disturbed. But the order of their stacking tells the story.

All along the east side of the park those Precambrian rocks, which are something more than a billion years old, lie flat on top of Cretaceous sedimentary rocks less than one tenth their age. That arrangement is exactly the opposite of the normal stacking, in which younger sedimentary rocks accumulate on top of older ones. In Glacier Park, as elsewhere in the Montana overthrust belt, the older rocks must have moved east onto the younger formations.

Watch the ancient Precambrian rocks in the high country of Glacier Park for marvelously preserved thin layers, sun-cracked mud surfaces, ripple marks, just about everything imaginable that could leave its mark in soft mud. Everything, that is, but some trace of animal life. No animals stirred those soft muds when they were laid down more than a billion years ago, there was no creature there to destroy the little prints we now see hardened into rock. But scummy growths of primitive blue-green algae abounded. We see their fossil remains in the rocks.

Layers of Cambrian limestone in the Chinese Wall. Abundant and varied animals first appeared on earth at the beginning of Cambrian time, about 600 million years ago. BRUCE SELYEM

Many rocks in Glacier Park contain curious structures that vaguely suggest fossil cabbages or Brussels sprouts. In fact, they are nothing of the kind. Those are the fossil remains of primitive blue-green algae, the very plants that began the long process of making the earth's atmosphere fit to breathe. Those algae may have been primitive, but they were green plants, and they did the green plant's business of absorbing carbon dioxide and giving off oxygen. Were it not for them and their more elaborate descendants, the earth's atmosphere would still be a suffocating blanket of carbon dioxide.

The Sawtooth Range

The Continental Divide follows long ridges south through the Sawtooth Range. Some of the rock formations in those ridges are much like those the Divide crosses in Glacier Park, others are younger sedimentary formations deposited during Paleozoic time, between 600 and 200 million years ago. Those rocks contain animal fossils, the remains of creatures that enjoyed the benefits of a breathable atmosphere.

The arrangements of the rocks in the Sawtooth Range is utterly different from that in Glacier Park, even though both areas are part of the overthrust belt. Instead of a single great slab that rode over the rocks beneath, the Sawtooth Range consists of many slabs stacked on each other like shingles on a roof.

At right: *Fossil blue-green algae in Precambrian limestone, Glacier National Park.* Far right: *Ripple marks in Precambrian sedimentary rock.* DAVE ALT PHOTOS

Imagine a great slab of rock encountering a rise as it moved east, moving up the ramp of the rise, then breaking at the base of the ramp instead of riding over the top. Then the broken end climbs the ramp, on top of the slab already there. That happened over and over, so the range now consists of a series of slabs each lapping onto the one ahead. All that happened sometime around 65 million years ago.

Since then, erosion has picked out the softer layers of rock to open the long valleys that trend from north to south through the Sawtooth Range. The parallel ridges are the more resistant formations standing up in relief. So the landscape of the Sawtooth Range expresses the arrangement of its rocks. Quite a lot of the erosion that picked out the long ridges and valleys happened since the streams began to flow between 2 and 3 million years ago.

Several large streams, such as the Sun River, cut right through those long ridges instead of following the valleys between them. Such canyons through the ridges are another legacy of the desert years. When the climate changed, the streams started flowing on a smooth and gently sloping desert surface above the level of the modern ridge crests. Then they encountered hard rocks that had been hidden beneath the surface as they began to erode their channels. But the streams were by then trapped in their valleys, with no alternative paths. They had to cut canyons through those ridges of hard rock because they could not flow uphill to escape their valleys and find an easier course over softer rock.

The Boulder Batholith and an Assortment of Volcanic Rocks

Between MacDonald Pass and Butte, the Continental Divide winds aimlessly through the Boulder Mountains. This is a broad tract of rugged hills deeply eroded into the granite of the Boulder batholith, its associated volcanic rocks and a deep pile of considerably younger volcanic rocks. The Divide continues across that assortment past the top of Starlight Mountain.

During the Cretaceous time, when the Boulder batholith was forming some 70 to 75 million years ago, the area between Helena and Butte was a vast volcanic field rather similar to the modern one in Yellowstone Park. It was one of those monsters among volcanoes called a "resurgent caldera." Those things typically go into major eruption at intervals measured in hundreds of thousands of years, and commonly produce dozens of cubic miles of lava in each

Frequent freezing and thawing crack the ancient and brittle Precambrian sedimentary rocks of the southern Bitterroot Range into unstable slopes cloaked with angular rubble. BILL CUNNINGHAM

large eruption. Geologists call the lava erupted from that volcano the Elkhorn Mountains volcanic rocks.

Meanwhile, even larger volumes of the same magma quietly crystallized into granite beneath the surface to become the Boulder batholith. The still-molten magma rose from its depths into the cover of volcanic rocks, then crystallized into pale gray granite. In many parts of the Boulder Mountains, we find hills composed of dark green volcanic andesite at the top, pale gray granite at the base. Bedrock exposures in those hills commonly reveal places where you can see fingers of granite penetrating the andesite. As different as they look, the volcanic rocks and granite have the same composition, so they must have formed from the same melt.

The last of the magma that fueled the big resurgent caldera finally crystallized about 70 million years ago, bringing the first phase of volcanic activity in the Boulder Mountains to a halt. Then the slow processes of erosion

gnawed through the volcanic pile, and into the granite beneath. By 50 million years ago, much of the volcanic rock was gone, and vast expanses of granite were laid bare. Then began the second phase of volcanic activity: eruption of the Lowland Creek volcanic pile.

In the Boulder Mountains, which lay right in the main volcanic trend of 50 million years ago, the eruptions produced large volumes of a white rock called rhyolite, along with lesser amounts of andesite. Most of these later andesites come in shades of reddish brown. They don't look much like the older greenish andesites formed from the granite of the Boulder batholith, nor do they have the same composition.

Since the volcanic activity of about 50 million years ago ended, erosion has stripped off much of the Lowland Creek volcanic rocks to again reveal the older andesite and granite beneath. Now, visitors to the Boulder Mountains see all three of those main types of rocks.

All the volcanic rocks contain closely spaced fractures that make exposures tend to break down into long slopes of sliding talus, the bane of hikers. The older andesites are typically rather dark greenish gray, and in many places they contain distinctive needles of glossy black hornblende. The younger Lowland Creek volcanic rocks tend to be some shade of brown if andesite, almost white if rhyolite. Both groups of volcanic rocks generally support a crust of dark lichens that completely cover the rock beneath, making it impossible to judge the color without looking at a freshly broken surface.

Fractures are widely spaced in the granite, so it tends to weather into large boulders that litter the surfaces of many slopes. Weathering also liberates iron oxides that stain the surfaces of the boulders reddish brown, and growths of lichens add touches of black. Those boulders form within the soil as the granite weathers preferentially along the widely spaced fractures. When erosion strips the soil off a slope, the boulders remain.

The Anaconda-Pintler Range

Between Starlight Mountain and Chief Joseph pass, the Continental Divide follows the Anaconda-Pintlar Range. Rocks in the eastern part of the range consist mostly of Precambrian sedimentary formations originally much like those in Glacier Park and the Sawtooth Range, now greatly recrystallized. Farther west, the range becomes mostly granite, part of the Idaho granite batholith. Geologically, this is the southern margin of the Sapphire block, one of the most remarkable parts of the northern Rocky Mountains.

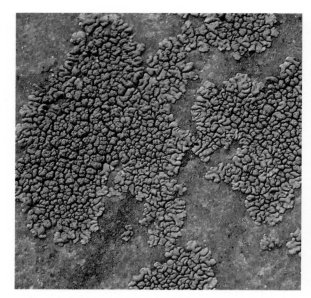

Right: *Fewer than 50 glaciers exist on Montana's Continental Divide—all in aptly named Glacier Park.* BRUCE SELYEM
Above: *Lichen can initiate the soil-building process even in nearly impervious granite as here in the West Big Hole.* BILL CUNNINGHAM

Top: *These scattered boulders were dropped exactly where we see them in Glacier's so-called 50-Mountain region as the glacier that was carrying them melted.* RICK GRAETZ.

Left: *The Chinese Wall, shown here near Larch Hill Pass, is a cliff of Cambrian limestone.* BILL CUNNINGHAM

Above: *Contorted layers of limestone exposed on Scapegoat Mountain.* BILL CUNNINGHAM

13

Weathered pinnacles of granite in the Highland Mountains south of Butte, part of the Boulder batholith. RICK GRAETZ

The Sapphire Block

Sometime between about 70 and 75 million years ago, a great slab of Idaho, the Sapphire block, slid about 50 miles east into Montana. The great mass of molten magma that finally became the granite of the Idaho batholith was still partly molten then, and the rocks above it simply sheared off. The detached slab was about 8 miles thick, in round numbers, and it probably moved east on a great smear of molten granitic magma, like a hot pancake sliding on melted butter. The Bitterroot Valley is the gap that opened behind the trailing edge of that slab. Many geologists guess that the whole movement may have happened in something like 2 or 3 million years. If so, then the slab moved an inch or two a year.

That massive slab of slowly moving rock bulldozed the rocks ahead of it into tight folds, many of which broke to become faults. And the leading edge of the slab also crumpled into tight folds. Meanwhile, the smear of molten granite magma beneath the moving slab leaked up along the faults and through the folds, then crystallized within them to form large masses of intrusive granite.

Now, we trace the margins of the Sapphire block by following its band of tight folds and faults with granite intrusions spiked into them through western Montana. Their path looks like a giant horseshoe laid on the map, its open end facing west. The southern edge of that horseshoe is the Anaconda-Pintler Range. If we trace it farther, we pass through the Flint Creek Range at the eastern edge of the horseshoe, and the Garnet Range along its northern edge.

The Southern Bitterroot Range

Between Chief Joseph Pass and Lemhi Pass, the Continental Divide follows the crest of the southern Bitterroot Range. Except for a few small masses of granite, almost all the rocks in that long march of mountains are Precambrian sedimentary formations basically similar to those the Divide crosses in the overthrust belt.

The Big Hole, a broad basin that spreads east from the southern Bitterroots to the high Pioneer Range, is probably just what its name suggests: a big hole in the earth's upper crust. It seems very likely that the Pioneer Range is another large block that, like the Sapphire block, detached from the Idaho batholith and moved east. If so, then the Big Hole is

the gap that opened behind that migratory piece of the crust. That probably happened about 75 million years ago, while the magma that eventually became the granite of the Idaho batholith was still at least partly molten. When it first opened, the Big Hole was also a deep hole.

Deep wells drilled in the Big Hole have penetrated some 14,000 feet of desert valley-fill sediment, mud, sand, gravel, volcanic ash and lake deposits. For untold millions of years, until it finally filled with sediment, a deep lake filled that basin.

The Beaverhead Range

Between Lemhi Pass and Monida Pass, the Divide follows the crest of the Beaverhead Range, as complex an assortment of much-abused rocks as any around. The north end of the range consists mostly of Precambrian sedimentary formations, all very tightly folded and broken along many faults. Rocks in the central and southern parts of the range include much younger sedimentary formations similarly deformed.

The Centennial Range

The Centennial Range splits the waters between Monida Pass and the area south of Raynolds Pass. Rocks there are a complex of tightly folded sedimentary formations covered in large areas by young volcanic rocks erupted within the last few million years, long after the folding was complete. The range arose like a big cellar door hinged at the south as the Centennial fault along its north face heaved it up. That fault is still moving, still raising the Centennial Range.

No one seems able to explain why the Centennial Range trends from east to west, approximately at right angles to the trends of other ranges in the region. Many geologists suspect that the answer may have something to do with the Snake River plain, the vast volcanic plateau that cuts a broad swath through Idaho to its active tip in the Yellowstone volcano. But the exact mechanism of the connection, if there is one, remains unclear.

From the east end of the Centennial Range, the Continental Divide jogs north to Raynolds Pass. Most of that part of its wanderings is across some of the oldest rocks in Montana. These are colorful metamorphic rocks, white marble, streaky gneiss, and platy schist full of glittering crystals. Most are rocks that formed deep within the earth's crust as older rocks recrystallized at red-hot temperatures and under extreme pressure. They recrystallized into metamorphic rocks sometime around 2.7 billion years ago, and there is no knowing how long the original rocks had been around before that.

Geologists call these ancient rocks "basement," because they lie beneath all other kinds of rocks and appear, for all that one can see at the surface, to continue to indefinite depth. We can tell from study of reflected earthquake waves that in most areas they extend downward to a depth of about 25 miles. Basement rocks are the continental crust itself. They exist everywhere beneath the continents, but in most areas they lie beneath a cover of younger sedimentary and volcanic rocks.

The Continental Divide continues across basement rocks for a few miles east of Raynolds Pass, then crosses tightly folded sedimentary rocks the rest of the way to Targhee Pass. These are more Paleozoic sedimentary rocks, deposited between 600 and 200 million years ago. Most of the formations accumulated in shallow water during one or another of the times that Montana was below sea level.

The Yellowstone Volcano

Between Targhee Pass and the end of our tour in Yellowstone Park, the Continental Divide crosses the western edge of the Yellowstone Plateau, across vast expanses of young volcanic rock. Most of it is rhyolite, pale volcanic rock with a composition similar to granite. It probably erupted from the Yellowstone Volcano, which is centered right in the middle of the park, sometime within the last 2 million years.

The Yellowstone Volcano doesn't look at all like the towering cones we normally summon to mind when we think of eruptions because it is not that type of volcano. It is a resurgent caldera, a real monster of a volcano, and there is no reason to suppose that it is dead.

The Yellowstone Volcano has produced three major eruptions at intervals of about 600,000 years, most recently about that long ago. That is a typical record for a resurgent caldera. Earthquake waves that pass beneath Yellowstone Park come out the other side lacking the kinds of wave motion that fail to pass through liquids. That leaves no doubt that a large mass of molten rock exists beneath the park, probably no more than a mile below the surface. Many of the small earthquakes in Yellowstone Park clearly show that the center of the volcano is rising. And some of the thermal areas are growing large and becoming hotter. The thing could erupt.

Resurgent calderas typically produce dozens of cubic miles of lava when they erupt. Most of that lava erupts

explosively as ash. Enormous steam explosions blast columns of ash high into the upper atmosphere, and spread blankets of red-hot ash over hundreds of square miles over the surrounding countryside. Most of the volcanic rocks between Targhee Pass and the park are that sort of volcanic overspray. Eruption of all that lava opens a yawning crater that later fills with lava as the eruptions continue.

No resurgent caldera has erupted in historic time, so we have no eyewitness accounts. But geologists have traced the blanket of ash from the last eruption of the Yellowstone Volcano all the way to south Texas. The sky must have been dark for weeks.

Some of the volcanic rocks in this neighborhood probably came from the Island Park Volcano, an older resurgent caldera immediately west of Yellowstone Park and south of the Continental Divide. The Island Park Volcano appears to be an older version of the Yellowstone Volcano that erupted for the last time several million years ago. As that eruption ended, the bottom of the crater filled with lava flows of black basalt. Half of the rim of that crater rises above the flows in a great ridge of pale rhyolite that follows an arc 28 miles in diameter. Since that last eruption, the Yellowstone Volcano has buried the eastern half of the Island Park Volcano under younger rhyolite.

Top: *The steep north face of the Centennial Range rose, and is still rising, along a fault.*
Bottom: *Phosphate mine in the Centennials.*
BILL CUNNINGHAM

15

Wandering to Three Seas

Picture a tiny snowflake falling on one slope of the Great Divide. Soon it becomes frozen in a snowbank with countless billions of its own kind. In the spring thaw it begins a timeless journey down a network of rills, sluices, rivulets, cataracts, creeks and other waterways until it adds a few molecules of moisture to the sea. That is, if it isn't drunk by a grizzly bear or a fir tree first. The Continental Divide has decided the destiny of this snowflake, whether it be the Gulf of Mexico, the Pacific Ocean, or faraway Hudson Bay.

There is nothing especially unusual about most divides. They are merely high ridges that separate the watersheds of rivers. Montana alone has thousands of small divides, separating the Bear Creeks from the Moose Creeks from the Willow Creeks. But nowhere on earth is there a divide of such grand dimensions — or one that parts the waters with such decisiveness — as the Great Divide.

Notably for Montana, almost all of the state's extensive surface water begins at the Continental Divide, except for the Kootenai drainage in the extreme northwestern corner of Montana and a few small closed basins east of the Divide.

This imperious watershed boundary divides not only rivers, but also oceans. On the Divide's east slope thousands of tiny tributaries eventually join to form the Missouri River, which flows into the Mississippi that twists for nearly 4,000 miles to the Gulf of Mexico. Down the more heavily-forested west slope plunge the Flathead, Blackfoot, Bitterroot, Clark Fork, and their thousands of lesser tributaries as they help fill the mighty Columbia on its journey to the Pacific.

These rivers existed before the mountains folded upward. When the land was flat, the rivers meandered lazily along silt-filled valleys. As the mountains lifted upward, the steeper gradients forced the streams out of their idle habits. We can thus trace the evolution of a river from its youth close to the Divide to its meandering maturity downstream.

Only a short distance from the crest of the continent below Glacier's Pollock Mountain, Lunch Creek has already gained considerable volume as it begins its descent to a great river far below. JEFF GNASS

A perpetual gift of life-giving water trickles from just below the summit of the Divide in the southern Bitterroot Range. BILL CUNNINGHAM

The quality, quantity and timing of runoff in southwest Montana's Big Hole River are determined by how the Continental Divide headwaters, shown in the background, are managed. RON GLOVAN

The infant streams near the Divide are short, often flowing intermittently but with great power after a heavy rain or the snowmelt of spring. The gradient of these high Divide watercourses may be so great that their gullies deepen after a single heavy rain.

Farther down the slope of the Divide, downward erosion slices into rock or ground that is wet all year (the water table), and the stream attains permanent flow. The narrow channel of the young brook continues to deepen, with rapids and waterfalls developing as the channel encounters layers of harder rocks. The steep valley is typically V-shaped.

The stream reaches maturity after it has begun to flow steadily, leaving the waterfalls and rapids behind. The bed of the river has widened as it swings from side to side in its channel, undercutting the outside and depositing sand on the inner bank. The shape of the valley begins to resemble a broad U with the gentle slopes of its walls rising to faraway ridges.

Far from the Divide, late maturity blends gradually into old age as the meanders become longer and the floodplain broader. During high water, the river will escape from its channel and flood the bottomlands, as the valley rises gently toward low hills.

Of course, not all precipitation that falls along or near the Divide begins its seaward journey as surface water. Moisture seeps into the soil by filling spaces between clay particles, and the fragments and grains of rock. The water moves lower until it meets the water table — a zone of wet rock where the spaces are filled with water. As the streams cut their gullies, they meet the uneven water table — thus tapping the earth's water storage container.

As precipitation is transformed into either surface or groundwater along the Divide, it assumes different forms for variable lengths of time. In some places along Montana's high crest it is stored in ancient glaciers, such as in the 40 or so living ice sculptures that hang close to the Divide in Glacier Park. In other places, water may rest briefly in icy cirque lakes, falling in stairstep fashion from lake to lake as it feeds downstream into the Columbia, Missouri or St. Mary Rivers. Along still other segments of the Divide, such as in many parts of the Bob Marshall, on

Nevada Mountain, and in the Centennials, the merging raindrops and snowflakes rush madly down steep channels without pause or rest, until reaching flatter water downstream.

During my meanderings along the even more meandering Divide in Montana, I have been most struck with the relative distinctiveness among its landscapes.

In some places, the Divide is truly heroic, as on the eastern brow of the Chinese Wall. There are other segments of the Divide in Glacier, the Anaconda-Pintlers, and the southern Bitterroot Range where a mountain goat would have trouble negotiating the knife-like ridges that separate the Atlantic from the Pacific. Here, one can literally see the continental waters dividing at one's feet. In other places, the Divide broadens into wide plateaus of alpine tundra, such as along the crest of the scenic Centennial Range just west of Yellowstone Park. In still other locations, the Divide abandons the highlands and winds indistinguishably through broad valleys, such as the Deer Lodge Pass area south of Butte. As I ventured along this varied watershed boundary, I sometimes had to search for that elusive dividing ridge.

17

Surface Water Along the Divide

In the mountains along and near the Divide, a high proportion of the annual precipitation falls during the winter snow-storage months. Snow-melt runoff in the mountains begins in April and typically peaks in late May or early June. The runoff is mostly complete in July, its progression toward low water somewhat modified by summer rains. Then, as precipitation picks up in the fall and plants use less water, another increase in water flow occurs before cold weather limits streamflow to the outflow rate of groundwater. The lowest sustained flows of mountain streams emanating from the Divide usually occur during March when groundwater outflow is at its lowest level.

Columbia-Pacific Basin

The Montana portion of the Columbia-Pacific Basin is located west of the Continental Divide. Because of the heavy, mostly orographic precipitation, this 17 percent of the state produces an astounding 58 percent of Montana's total stream flow. Annual precipitation varies widely throughout the basin, from around 15 inches in the lower valleys to about 120 inches along the Divide in Glacier Park. The range in elevation within the basin is as dramatic as the difference in precipitation. From the 10,000-foot summits along the Divide, the drainage drops rapidly to the lowest point in Montana — the 1,820' elevation of the Kootenai River where it crosses into Idaho.

The upper Columbia River basin in western Montana is composed of two major river systems. The Kootenai River drains the northwestern corner of Montana from its source in British Columbia some 130 miles north of the international boundary. The other system is the Clark Fork-Flathead.

The Clark Fork River originates in Montana along the Continental Divide. It joins with the Flathead River near Plains, Montana, and flows northwest from the state as the Clark Fork. All but 450 of the 9,000 square miles of Flathead River drainage lie within Montana. The North Fork originates in British Columbia, but both the Middle and South Forks have headwaters along remote stretches of the Divide in the Bob Marshall Wilderness country. The average annual flow of the Flathead at its mouth exceeds that of the Missouri where it leaves Montana, even though the latter's drainage area is ten times larger.

The emerald green pools of the east-side Dearborn River originate from snow banks hanging along the Divide deep within the pristine watersheds of the Scapegoat Wilderness. BILL CUNNINGHAM

Although proposals for dams on the forks of the Flathead have been advanced over the years, some 214 miles of its three forks were added to the National Wild and Scenic Rivers System in 1976. This special federal legislation protects the free-flowing wilderness waterways from impoundment.

Missouri-Atlantic Basin

The upper Missouri basin in Montana drains about 82 percent of the state and provides approximately 40 percent of the state's total streamflow. The Missouri, formed by the confluence of the Jefferson, Madison and Gallatin Rivers at Three Forks, flows through northeastern Montana and into North Dakota. Its major Continental Divide tributaries below Three Forks are the Dearborn, Sun, Teton, Marias and Milk Rivers. The Milk begins in Montana, flows north into Canada, and then heads southeastward back into Montana.

The western and southwestern parts of the upper Missouri Basin, near its Continental Divide headwaters, are in the Northern Rocky Mountain physiographic province. Annual precipitation varies widely from 100 inches along the Divide in Glacier Park to about 11 inches in some of the intermontane valleys east of the Divide. The differences in elevations east of the Divide are comparable to those of the west side — from more than 11,000' in the Italian Peaks of southwest Montana to only 1,880' where the Missouri leaves the state. But the "leveling out" distances are not at all comparable. The Kootenai River's exit from Montana is only about 200 miles west of the Divide, whereas the Missouri requires nearly 700 miles to descend to about the same elevation on the high plains of eastern Montana.

St. Mary-Hudson Bay Basin

About one percent of Montana is contained within the uppermost reaches of the Hudson Bay drainage, within and adjacent to the northeastern corner of Glacier Park. This watershed area produces about 2 percent of the state's total streamflow. The major river in the basin is the St. Mary, which flows northward from Glacier Park into Canada to the Saskatchewan River and then into the icy waters of Hudson Bay.

A group of citizens gathered on a damp spring day at the remote site of a proposed natural gas exploratory well three miles south of Glacier Park in Lewis and Clark Forest's Badger-Two Medicine roadless area. They were expressing concern about the impact of energy development on wildlife, the park, and the local tourism-based economy. But it took former Blackfeet Tribal Council member Dan Boggs to drive home a central point. "This is the very headwaters of our nation," said Boggs as he pointed southwest toward Elkcalf Mountain and the Continental Divide. "If we degrade the headwaters up here there is no hope for those downstream."

Indeed, as more and more proposals for logging, mining, energy development and roading are advanced for presently wild but unprotected segments of Montana's Divide, we must recognize their effects on all downstream waters. Unless appropriate stretches of the high crest are preserved, and other sections carefully managed, we risk grave consequences to the quality of the nation's major waterways.

But for now, at least, the message is one of hope. The continual gifts of Montana's wild, remote Continental Divide are birth, renewal and life. For next spring, that tiny snowflake will become part of a seep, a trickle, a gush, a great free river bound for a distant sea.

*From where the Divide forms the most distant point of the 4,000-mile-long Missouri/Mississippi river system. The same dividing ridge is visible some 20 miles northeast, atop the Mt. Henry/Lionhead Mountains.*BILL CUNNINGHAM

Hellroaring Creek: Most Distant Source of the Muddy Mo

It was a wet Sunday afternoon on August 11. I had finished up a weekend tour in the Centennials and was determined to find and photograph the most distant source of the Missouri River from its mouth — the extreme head of Hellroaring Creek in the east end of the rugged Centennial Mountains just south of Red Rock Pass. As the weather grew increasingly foreboding, my determination to hike the steep ten miles to the start of Hellroaring Creek increased — combining stubbornness and lack of good sense. I decided to make it as far up the drainage as possible that afternoon with only a light camp, saving discovery of the actual source for the next morning.

Confident that the weather could only improve, I had set off at 4 p.m. dressed for speed in only a flimsy rain slick, and running shoes and shorts — defying the driving rain that was now slamming full force into my face. I trudged up an unmaintained, overgrown trail as the rain turned to hail and soon gave way to heavy, wet snow. Four miles farther, I finally succumbed to the idea of pitching camp along a series of open, parklike benches on the west side of the creek. Already, my feet were beginning to freeze inside my soaking wet running shoes. The storm continued to unleash its fury most of the night. By morning the clouds parted just enough to briefly display a gleaming mantle of new snow on Mt. Jefferson — the highest Continental Divide point in the Centennials at 10,196'.

My world was one of unending wet and cold on that dark dawn. Instead of touching the ultimate source of the Missouri, I had to satisfy myself with merely photographing it from a distance above camp. the unrelenting rain drove me out of the country as I slogged back to my car through mud and dripping brush.

I was not to be undone by the combined forces of foul weather, tough terrain and long distances. Three weeks later I again embarked on an expedition to the most distant origin of the Missouri River. My goal was once more threatened by ominous dark clouds and high winds, but at least there was no fresh, wet snow decorating my raincoat.

This time I found a much easier route to the extreme head of Hellroaring Creek along southwest Montana's Great Divide. I drove almost to the top of Sawtell Mountain just northwest of Island Park, Idaho, and hiked an old sheep driveway for about 2½ miles to the Continental Divide just above Hellroaring Creek. I was impressed by the modest beginnings of so great a river, as I observed the dry gullies and long-since-melted snow glades hanging along the crest. Winding through some ten miles of remote, roadless meadow and canyon country, Hellroaring Creek soon joins the Red Rock River, then the Beaverhead, the Big Hole, the Jefferson and on to the official start of the Missouri River at Three Forks.

Interbasin Water Transfers

Piping water from one watershed and over a divide into another is called an interbasin water transfer. There are two such transfers in Montana, both of waters close to the Continental Divide.

The oldest interbasin water diversion dates back to 1899 when the Butte Water Company completed a pumping station on the Big Hole River at the town of Divide. The next year water was pumped more than 800 vertical feet over the Continental Divide and then some 20 miles north to Butte. Despite an expansion of the system, some of the original redwood stave pipe still is in service.

Montana's other interbasin transfer is the 29-mile-long St. Mary Canal just northeast of Glacier Park. This canal carries an average seasonal flow of 175,000 acre-feet from the St. Mary River across the Hudson Bay Divide into the North Fork of the Milk River. The Boundary Waters Treaty of 1909 between the United States and Canada is the basis for the apportionment of water from the St. Mary and Milk Rivers. The additional flow from the St. Mary into the Milk helps satisfy the need for extensive downstream irrigation between Havre and Glasgow. However, there is growing concern about water shortages in this part of Montana because of an increased water demand in the lower reaches of the Milk, combined with Canada's increased use of its apportioned share.

These two longstanding diversions merely redistribute water within Montana. As such, they have not been as controversial as proposed projects that would transfer water out of the state.

Left: *Signing the register atop 8,020' Triple Divide Peak where water is spilled into three continental watersheds. Far below lies the cirque basin of Hudson Bay Creek.* BRUCE SELYEM
Above: *From the head of Atlantic Creek, Triple Divide Peak (on left) stands out as a sharply jutting spur of Norris Mountain—a Continental Divide summit to the northwest.* BILL CUNNINGHAM

I knew that if I reached no other point on the Great Divide, Triple Divide Peak had to be it. My long-awaited ascent up the scenic, heavily-forested Cutbank Creek drainage to Atlantic Creek was immediately preceded by a mid-August storm that dropped up to six inches of wet snow on the peaks. Luckily, our 7½-mile journey by good trail to Triple Divide Pass was marked by clear, cool weather with not a cloud in the brilliant blue sky. I decided not to scramble up the steep summit ridge directly southwest of the pass. Instead, I found an easier but longer route to the south at the head of Atlantic Creek. By mid-afternoon I stood atop the nation's only true triple divide, viewing the rugged ridgelines that marked the three great continental watersheds. At this unique point I was touching the only junction of three major North American divides: the Hudson Bay-Atlantic, the Atlantic-Pacific, and the Pacific-Hudson Bay. I was humbled and awe-struck by the thought that I was standing atop the beginning of three of the largest and longest river systems in the Northern Hemisphere: the Missouri-Mississippi, the Columbia, and the Saskatchewan-Nelson.

The water of Atlantic Creek begins its journey as snowmelt from the crown of Triple Divide Peak, pauses briefly in Grizzly Medicine Lake, and then resumes its rapid tumble to Cutbank Creek and on to the mighty Missouri. BILL CUNNINGHAM

Norris Mountain sends streams of snowmelt thousands of feet down sheer cliff walls into the lush, open meadows of the Basin. Across the Divide to the north are several tarns at the head of Hudson Bay Creek. Portions of these north-facing lakes normally stay frozen year-round. The barren glacial moraines and tarn lakes of the upper basin soon give way to the broad, open drainage of Hudson Bay Creek as it flows northward into Red Eagle Lake and onto expansive St. Mary Lake. On the east side of Triple Divide Peak, Atlantic Creek begins as a series of green shelves. These parallel strips of green amidst huge piles of rock talus and glacial debris become soaked by the snowmelt and emerging springs that feed off the Divide. Soon the waters are plunging off cliffs into the cirque basin of deep blue Medicine Grizzly Lake. Beyond is a classic U-shaped valley leading to the main Cutbank Creek drainage, scoured by the glaciers that have left their marks everywhere on the face of Glacier Park.

Because Triple Divide Peak offers unobstructed views of three large alpine basins, the view from the top exceeds that of many nearby peaks that are a thousand or more feet higher. Triple Divide is actually a sharply-jutting spur of a Continental Divide peak to the northwest, 8,882' Norris Mountain. But as the starting point for three of the world's great watersheds, what an important spur it is!

Triple Divide: Timeless Sentinel of Three Ocean Watersheds

Whatever can be said about the Continental Divide, the only absolute is that it separates a vast continent between great ocean watersheds. Thus, the single most notable point along the tens of thousands of miles of its length, let alone its 800 or so miles in Montana, may be 8,020' Triple Divide Peak in southern Glacier National Park. From its crown, water drains down Atlantic Creek and eventually some 4,000 miles to the Gulf of Mexico. Across the Hudson Bay Divide to the north, water plummets into a creek by the same name, eventually to reach frigid Hudson Bay. Bounded by the 49th Parallel on the north, the Continental Divide to the west, and the Hudson Bay Divide trending northeast, is that 650-square-mile, one percent of Montana that comprises the uppermost reaches of the Hudson Bay watershed. Toward the southwest, Triple Divide Peak gives birth to Pacific Creek, which ultimately mixes with the blue Pacific at the mouth of the mighty Columbia River. No other peak in the United States and only one other point in North America feeds waters into three faraway seas.

The head of each drainage basin is quite different from the other two. Unlike its counterparts to the north and east, the upper Pacific Creek basin is devoid of alpine lakes.

Not All Triple Divides Are Created Equal

There are actually two Triple Divide Peaks along the Continental Divide in Montana. The other is in a remote southern corner of the Bob Marshall Wilderness a few miles northwest of massive Scapegoat Mountain. Don't confuse the true triple divide of three ocean watersheds in Glacier Park with its 8,450' namesake in the Bob. The Bob Marshall counterpart contributes water to the Gulf of Mexico-Atlantic Ocean by means of a nameless tributary to the South Fork of the Sun River. From the west side of the peak, the Pacific Ocean receives water through two drainages: the Bar Creek tributary to the Danaher River, and high sources of the Dry Fork North Fork of the Blackfoot River.

Combat Zone
of
Montana's Weather

Moisture-laden clouds pour from the Great Divide in Glacier Park as surely as the spring runoff. CHARLES KAY

There's a saying in Montana that if you don't like the weather just wait for an hour or so; it's bound to change. Along the Continental Divide you probably won't have that long a wait. The singular characteristic of Montana's high crest that has most impressed me is its constantly changing topography which, in turn, contributes to dramatic and often changeable weather. During my various treks along the Divide in preparation for this book it seemed as though there was a new weather surprise around every bend in that serpentine mountain barrier. Intense, high-altitude sun at 11,000 feet during February; heavy, wet snow and bone-chilling winds in Glacier during mid-August; torrential rain near the Chinese Wall in early September; you name it and the Divide served it up with flair, drama and unpredictability.

Indeed, weather is the arbiter of life in Continental Divide country. It exercises this power in a dazzling array of changing moods of wind, rain, snow, sleet, heat and cold. At one moment it may bring gentle breezes and warm rain that foster life, and then with shattering abruptness bring fierce winds and intense cold that clutches plants and animals in a death-like grip.

Montana weather comes from a westerly direction (an arc from NW to SW) about 90 percent of the time. The Continental Divide serves as a continuous, unbroken barrier at right angles to these prevailing winds.

Summers tend to be warm and dry. Thunderstorms are more frequent west of the Divide because of the mountainous terrain, even though east of the Divide the air is often warmer and the humidity higher.

In late August to mid-September one can almost count on a week or two of unsettled, stormy weather in the mountain regions of the Divide. After this interlude, a large high-pressure ridge typically builds over the Northern Rockies with clear, dry air, warm days and cold nights often extending into late October. By November, the snowpack is building in the valleys on both sides of the Divide.

As winter envelops the country, storms increase, especially west of the Divide. The bitter cold on the east side is occasionally broken by a warm chinook wind. January through early March brings longer periods of clear, cold weather. At the higher elevations of the Divide, the precipitation is more evenly distributed throughout the year than at lower elevations. The accumulation of winter snow, which can vary between 50 percent and 170 percent of "average," has a big effect on runoff since about 70 percent of the spring and summer streamflow emanating from the Divide comes from winter and spring snow. Snowpack is a marvelously designed natural water storage system, which is nature's way of storing unneeded precipitation in winter for when it is needed in the summer.

Winter travelers along the steep terrain of Montana's Continental Divide must keep a wary eye out for the "white death" of avalanches. These massive slides can carry thousands of tons of snow at speeds greater than 100 miles per hour. The intense air blasts in front of the avalanche can snap large trees like toothpicks. The danger is usually greatest during and after winter storms, and during snowmelt. Avalanche conditions along the Divide may persist for weeks during long periods of bitter cold.

As spring approaches, March storms may be a combination of arctic and spring snowstorms. This mixing of systems may produce the most severe storms of the year, with below-zero temperatures, heavy snows and strong winds. With the advent of spring, the strong westerly flow from the Pacific weakens compared to the late fall and winter months. This opens Montana's weather gate to subtropical moisture from the Gulf of Mexico. The east slopes of the Divide, usually dry with the westerlies, become wet as gulf moisture moves north and then rides on easterly winds to the Divide.

By mid-May the rainy season becomes most pronounced east of the Divide. June is the wettest month, followed by May, along the lower slopes of Montana's Divide. One exception is Marias Pass where the wettest months are November, December and January because of the heavy snowfall. And so we find ourselves back to the fleeting summer of Divide country — the warm period of late July and early August when most of the precipitation falls as showers during thunderstorms.

Montana Weather Zones Along the Continental Divide

Four of Montana's nine forecast zones abut the Continental Divide, with the Divide generally being the boundary between the Northwestern and West Central Zones (1 and 2) on the west side and the Northwest Chinook and Southwestern Zones (3 and 4) to the east.

The Northwestern zone is the wettest. The heaviest yearly normal precipitation measured in this zone is 39.22 inches at Marias Pass on the Divide. Most of the precipitation falls during the period of strongest westerlies, from November through February. Sometimes, this Pacific moisture pattern is altered when subtropical moisture crosses over the Divide from the east as a result of large-scale easterly storm systems.

To the south, the West Central Zone has the mildest winter temperatures in the state. On rare occasions, a deep invasion of cold arctic air may spill into the area through Rogers Pass at the head of the Big Blackfoot River on the Divide. Strong westerlies tend to carry precipitation over

Weather Forecast Zones

1 Northwestern Montana	**4** Southwestern Montana	**7** South Central Montana
2 West Central Montana	**5** North Central Montana	**8** Northeastern Montana
3 Northwest Chinook Zone	**6** Central Montana	**9** Southeastern Montana

the valleys, dumping the moisture on the mountains along and to the west of the Divide.

The Northwest Chinook Zone is truly the combat zone between the arctic and Pacific air masses. The battle extends from around the first of November until April. The relief map tells it all. Here there is an abrupt change from the plains to the mountains along the Divide that extends well into Alberta. As cold, dense arctic air flows south from Alberta into northern Montana, its westward movement is often stopped by the Rocky Mountain Front, which closely parallels the Divide.

Oscillations of the arctic front just east of the Divide cause dramatic temperature changes. The 100-degree drop in 24 hours at Browning on January 23 and 24, 1916, still stands as a national record.

The southwestern zone has the greatest variety of climates. The valleys, which lie east of the Divide, are shielded from precipitation by the surrounding mountains. The valleys in this zone are the highest in the state and exhibit huge temperature drops at night when the sky clears and the valley is snow-covered. During the summer, this zone spawns numerous thunderstorms, which develop in the afternoon over the mountains and typically spread northeastward from the Divide.

Variables in Continental Divide Weather

The three major variables influencing weather along the mountainous Divide are exposure to the sun, topographic relief and, most of all, elevation.

As the coldest temperatures of the day are reached near sunrise, the eastern summits of the Divide are just receiving the first warmth. Farther down the slopes the sun's heat comes slowly or not at all. South-facing slopes will be warmest throughout the day, but they never get as much heat as the summits. Many of the sheltered north-facing slopes of the Divide are encased in shadow as the sun is setting. That is why snowbanks persist on high north and northeastern slopes, even when warm summer winds are blowing.

Morning and evening breezes in the mountains are often the result of local topographic contours along the Divide rather than from major wind systems. In the evening, the cool air drains down into the valleys lowering the temperatures. The next day the sun warms the mountain slopes. The heated air rises and is replaced by the valley air, creating a daytime breeze out of the valley toward the high crest.

Pacific air masses moving over western Montana are forced to rise over the Rockies toward the Continental Divide. They cool as they lift, and thus their capacity to hold moisture decreases. The resulting mountain-induced precipitation caused by the rising topography is called "orographic." The amount of precipitation tends to increase at higher elevations west of the Divide, with the maximum occurring along the crest. As the air masses top the Divide and move down the east side they warm and are again able to hold more moisture. Thus, we see the "rainshadow" effect being most pronounced along the dry east slopes and valleys adjacent to the Divide. This pattern of orographic precipitation over the highlands with dry valleys lying in their rainshadow is repeated several times because the Montana Rocky Mountain chain is not a single high ridge, but rather, a series of ranges. The rainshadow effect immediately east of the Divide is most dramatic north of Helena because this segment of the Divide is part of a more continuous mountain mass close to the front wall of the Rockies. The air thus drops abruptly to the plains. South of Helena, the Rockies are broken into a series of mountain ranges separated by large, intermountain valleys that are within the rainshadows of ranges to their west.

Left: *Near the Rocky Mountain Front the Continental Divide pierces an ocean of thick clouds.* LARRY MAYER
Right: *Summertime in the Rockies—fickle Divide weather turns wintry during an early August snowstorm in the southern Bitterroots.* BILL CUNNINGHAM

How the Great Divide Influences Weather in Montana

The Continental Divide is like any other mountain range in its influence on weather. The key difference is that the Divide is a more or less unbroken barrier to the prevailing westerlies that have to cross it. Literally the climax of the orographic precipitation process, it is the end point of the continuous climb of the moist Pacific air mass. This pattern of warmer, drier air sliding down the east slopes of the Divide and the resulting rainshadow effect are most pronounced during the cold season from fall to mid-spring. During the summer the air is already warm so the extra lift of rising over the Divide instead spurs the development of thunderstorms.

The Continental Divide is also a barrier to the westward movement of cold arctic air. Arctic air often moves south along the Rocky Mountain Front from Canada like a surge of water after a dam break. Usually the dense cold air mass isn't deep enough to spill over the Divide to the west. In fact, the most significant effect of the Continental Divide on the west side is the protection it normally provides from the cold arctic air that rolls down from the north. However, several times a winter the cold air mass becomes deep enough to slop over Marias Pass and several other low points on the Divide. As the cold, heavy air literally rolls down the western slopes of the Divide severe blizzard conditions can occur. The dreaded Hellgate winds of Missoula and the nearly 100-mile-per-hour wind blasts through the narrow gorge of the Flathead River Canyon just east of Columbia Falls result from these conditions.

South of Helena, the Continental Divide exerts much less effect on weather. Its identity as a weather barrier is diminished because there are several higher mountain ranges to the east. Occasionally, there is a local anomaly that defies the usual rainshadow effect east of the Divide. A case in point is the lush Elkhorn Mountain Range located a short distance east of the Divide southeast of Helena. The Elkhorn Range receives abundant moisture, compared to far drier nearby ranges, because it is higher than the Continental Divide to the west and because the continuous mountain mass between it and the Divide prevents the downslope rainshadow effect that is so evident in nearby Helena Valley.

On the east side, the Divide can have a major influence on spring flooding. Flooding east of the Divide simply does not occur from snowmelt alone. From spring to early fall, subtropical moisture from the Gulf of Mexico may swing up to the Divide via upslope easterly winds. Upon reaching the mountains the air rises rapidly and abruptly more than 4,000 feet.

Much of the moisture from the storm drops within a short distance compared to Pacific storms that gradually lose their moisture over much longer distances. In these upslope storms the air may actually be more moist than Pacific masses because the subtropical air is much warmer than that that arrives from the colder Northwest coast. Since these heavy rains occur during May and June, which is also the time of heavy snowmelt runoff, major spring flooding can occur on the east side. The effect of the Divide is most pronounced where it coincides with the Front Range on the eastern slopes. During these flood-prone conditions, the storm center is to the south as was the case with the destructive 1964 floods. Here the rains are heaviest along the Divide, and do not extend far to the west.

Differences in temperature on both sides of the Divide are greatest during the winter, with variations of 50 to 60 degrees being fairly common. But sometimes the differences are not in the direction that you might expect. During the severe winter of 1968-1969 West Yellowstone, often the nation's deep freeze, was among the warmest places in Montana. This was because the cold air was not deep enough to cross the high terrain north of West Yellowstone and the Continental Divide. The same was true of mile-high Butte, just west of the Divide, which uncharacteristically remained much warmer than nearby Helena, which is located just east of MacDonald Pass. Again, the cold air wasn't deep enough to slop over the Divide. On at least one occasion, the gaslines of a bus actually froze when it entered the abrupt transition zone between balmy Butte and frigid Helena.

National Weather Service meteorologist Grayson Cordell tells of a time during the winter back in the 1960s when the temperature along the Divide at Summit was fluctuating so rapidly that it could not be tracked. The temperature shifted that day at least 15 times between -20 and 40 degrees. This rapid and constant shifting occurred at the interface between cold arctic air and warm maritime air at Marias Pass. The cold and warm air masses could not mix because of the large differences in their densities.

Orographic winter precipitation is sufficient to pile deep layers of snow along much of Montana's Divide country. Snow depths can rise to more than 800 inches in the sheltered cirque basins of the leeward eastern slopes of the southern Bitterroot Range. Precipitation measurements in Glacier Park's Grinnell Basin over an 11-year period averaged an astounding 147 inches per year. Some readings were up to 180 inches. The more favored northeast-facing slopes abutting the Divide may exceed 200 inches of precipitation per year. According to the measured average for this portion of the Divide, the annual snowfall exceeds 1,000 inches. Don't expect to pitch your winter tent on bare ground here unless you plan to dig through 80 feet of snow! It's easy to see why winter is the wettest season of the year along this northern reach of the Divide. Farther downslope to the east the wet season shifts to May and June.

Wind is a constant companion along the Continental Divide. When it isn't snowing, the wind is churning dry, gritty snow into blinding blizzards. It's little wonder that some of the local folks just east of the Divide claim that not much snow falls, but a lot blows through. What does fall, doesn't melt — it just blows around until it wears out.

When people think of windy places in Montana, Livingston automatically comes to mind. However, the Marias Pass area is likely the wind capital of the state with the funneling effect of the terrain and because of its proximity to the northern storm centers. Winds are strongest as they move downslope near the center of a low pressure system. The northern stretches of Montana's Continental Divide are the windiest along the Divide because they are closest to the mean storm track. Several years ago a weather observer near the northern Continental Divide on the east side called the Great Falls office and exclaimed, "It's so windy that I can't keep the water in my toilet!"

Of all the winds that blow along Montana's Divide, there are none more dramatic than the fabled chinooks, or "snow-eaters" as the Indians called them. The chinook, or "foehn" as it is known in the Alps, is a warm, dry downslope wind that occurs on the downwind, eastern slopes of the Continental Divide. The chinook is born in mild, wet winds that rise up the western slopes of the Divide, cooling until the moisture is wrung from the air. The condensation process in the formation of precipitation adds heat to the air. As the wind starts down the eastern slopes of the Divide it is warmed further by the decreasing altitude, until it arrives along the Rocky Mountain Front as a dry, warm wind.

The effects of the chinook winds are most spectacular in winter when bitter cold invades Montana. As the warm chinook front moves through the country dramatic temperature rises occur. Examples in the chinook belt include a rise of 43 degrees in 15 minutes, from -6 to 37 degrees, and an increase of 26 degrees in 45 seconds, from 16 to 42 degrees.

Just as dramatic is the sound of an oncoming chinook front heard from within the mountain canyons. Its roar sounds like a freight-train is bearing down through the downslope canyons.

Chinook-savvy ranchers along the eastern slopes look for characteristic chinook clouds above the mountains that seem to be "boiling" in the wind but remain stationary. When this happens, moisture is evaporating as the air moves down the east side. From this condition, they often can predict a chinook before it hits.

The importance of the Divide on the development of chinooks is a function of the terrain north of Helena and the fact that the northern Divide almost touches the plains in places. Chinooks occur by the same principles south of Helena, but not so often nor so dramatically. Here the Divide is in the interior of the mountain chains as opposed to being closer to the eastern edge of the Rockies farther north.

The Great Divide frequently displays the most severe weather in a state that has a national reputation for severe weather. The weather reaches extremes, with high winds, heavy precipitation, bitter cold, and clouds that often contain super-cooled water that freezes instantly on contact. Because of severe icing it is almost impossible to maintain wind measuring equipment on top of the Divide.

Montana's Continental Divide climate is wily, fast-moving, changeable, abrupt and unpredictable. It is influenced by contrasting pressure systems and their related summer and winter weather patterns. The Divide literally makes its own weather by means of deflections caused by its unbroken mountain barrier, and the elevations with which the prevailing westerlies must cope. The varied moods and faces of the Great Divide, highlighted by changeable weather during each of the seasons, go to the very essence of what Montana's windswept crest is all about.

Tragedy struck on the Divide in June 1962 when a missionary family of four from Washington State lost their lives in a light plane crash about one mile northeast of 9,202' Scapegoat Mountain, a few yards below the crest of the Continental Divide. Scapegoat looms above the wreckage in the background. It took three days to locate the remote site of the mishap in a wild country so vast that several other downed planes have yet to be found. BILL CUNNINGHAM

With the crest of the Great Divide in the background, super-cold air has settled into the Big Hole Valley for a long winter. BILL CUNNINGHAM

70 Below and Falling

You won't hear the Chamber of Commerce bragging about it, but during the early morning of January 20, 1954, a national record was established next to the Continental Divide just west of Rogers Pass. It was there that the cold temperature for the lower 48 states of minus 70 degrees F. was observed at a mining camp. The mine was located at an elevation of 5,470 feet.

This record-setting plunge of the mercury was observed by H.M. Kleinschmidt, a National Weather Service cooperative observer. Although the record low occurred on January 20, the State Climatologist at the Weather Bureau was not aware of it until about February 3 when January's weather data were received in Helena. Kleinschmidt was then asked to send his thermometer in to be checked.

He sent in both the official minimum thermometer as well as his own alcohol thermometer. The observer wrote that he was kept up most of the bitterly cold night by loud and constant "popping" noises in his cabin. About 2 a.m. he looked at his thermometer located outside an insulated window. It indicated minus 68 degrees. He then went to the official weather measurement shelter and discovered that the minimum thermometer read colder than minus 65 degrees, which was the lowest point on the scale. The index had actually retreated into the bulb.

A laboratory check by the Weather Bureau in Washington, D.C., under conditions exactly as described by the observer confirmed the minus 70 reading. Indeed, the conditions had been right for an extreme low temperature. The high altitude weather station was situated in a saucer-shaped depression. During the preceding week, Montana had been invaded several times by extremely frigid arctic air. A solid week of heavy snow had increased the snow

depth at the mine from eight inches to 66 inches. The windless, crystal clear night was perfect for super-cooling.

All we know for sure on that incredibly frigid night is that the temperature dropped to *at least* minus 70 degrees. The mercury likely would have continued to plummet had the thermometer been able to record its nadir since the 70-below-zero reading occurred at 2 a.m. even though the lowest temperature of the night usually happens just after sunrise.

We will continue to see challenges to this Montana Continental Divide record from other Rocky Mountain states. Utah recorded a close but unsuccessful attempt in 1985. But the lowest recorded temperature in the continental United States at Rogers Pass will stand until all of the extreme conditions come together at a weather station in an extreme location. Two other ingredients will be necessary: a colder reading thermometer and some hardy soul willing to observe it!

BILL CUNNINGHAM

Temperature Records

Lowest -70 degrees F., Rogers Pass, January 20, 1954 (national record)

Greatest Change in 24 hours From 44 degrees F. to -56 degrees F., Browning (just east of Continental Divide), January 23, 1916 (national record)

Precipitation Record (statewide record)

Greatest in One Year 55.51 inches, Summit (Marias Pass on Continental Divide), 1953 (statewide record at a measuring station)

Snowfall Records (statewide records)

Greatest in 24 hours 44.0 inches, Summit, January 20, 1972

Greatest in one storm 77.5 inches, Summit, January 17-22, 1972

These official recorded extremes illustrate the truth of the saying that there is no "normal" weather, just extremes averaged into a normal. One can only speculate about the record extremes that must occur along high, austere portions of the Divide where there are no certified intruments or stalwart weather observers available to make the recordings.

The great barrier of the Divide in the southern Bitterroot Range is not enough to protect this and other alpine lakes from the potentially disastrous effects of acid rain. BILL CUNNINGHAM

Acid Moisture Along the Divide

Before the era of modern transportion, the Continental Divide was a barrier to westward migration, an imposing obstacle to be overcome. Even today, this formidable dividing ridge of the Rockies discourages all but the most persistent storms from dropping their precipitation on the drier east side. But even this great topographic uplift is not enough to protect the most remote reaches of Montana's Divide from the effects of acid rain and snowfall.

During the winter of 1985, I took several back-country ski trips in the Pintlers, southern Bitterroots, Italian Peaks, Centennials and other wilderness stretches of Montana's Continental Divide. I didn't fully realize at the time that the outwardly pristine snow blanketing this high country may harbor the hidden pollution of acid precipitation.

There is a proven connection between acid rain and snow and emissions from industrial plants and cars. This condition occurs when sulphur dioxide and nitrogen oxides from these sources lift into the atmosphere and mix with cloud moisture to form mild solutions of sulphuric and nitric acids. Winds carry these solutions for hundreds of miles before they fall as acid rain or snow.

There are places along the Divide in southwestern Montana where the snow is excessively acidic according to mountain snow sampling by the U.S. Soil Conservation Service. Clean snow has a slightly acidic pH of 5.6, but some tested on the Montana side of the Bitterroot Range near the Divide displayed a highly acidic pH of 4.0. Similar to the seismic readings, a drop in the pH by one point means a tenfold increase in acidity.

Acid precipitation is a deadly killer of lakes, as documented in the Adirondack Mountains of upstate New York. Here, animal and plant life have been destroyed in scores of lakes. Many areas along the Divide are underlain by granitic or basaltic rocks, which are low in natural buffers like carbonates. With no way to neutralize the acid, the mountain lakes in these areas are highly vulnerable to acidification. As the waters become more acidic the first victims are fish eggs, following by frogs and bacteria. The last to go are adult fish, which absorb heavy metals, such as mercury, that are leached from the rocks by the acidic water.

Forest productivity also may be decreased if trees are exposed to acid precipitation for long periods. Of more direct concern to people is the possibility that heavy metals may be leached into domestic water supplies by acid-laden moisture.

Acid pollution may be crossing over Montana's Divide from the southwest, southern California and the Salt Lake City area. While the problem may not yet be severe, it is certainly a threat to some remote high-mountain lakes near the Divide. Careful monitoring and enforcement of national air pollution standards in metro areas is imperative if we are to avoid long-term ecological damage to the headwaters of our nation's water supplies.

Tale of the Timberline

Much of Montana's Continental Divide consists of a high, dividing ridge above timberline separating the watersheds of two great oceans. Images of high elevation rock and ice abound, although one cannot so neatly categorize the ever-changing sweep of the Great Divide. Because of these popular images of an austere treeless landscape, vegetation is certainly not the first natural resource that comes to mind when the Divide is mentioned.

Nonetheless, as a topographical barrier to weather patterns, the Divide has a profound influence on vegetation, both east and west. As we examine the Divide from Glacier National Park south to Yellowstone we are confronted with an amazing array of vegetative diversity, from glaciers and wind-blown rocks where scarcely a lichen can grow, to lush maritime forests. However, all along the Divide including the jagged horn peaks of Glacier, the magnificent Chinese Wall, the crags of the Anaconda-Pintlers and the southern Bitterroots, most of the Divide can be characterized as landscapes at or near timberline. Steve Arno's *Timberline* provided much of the background for assessing the influence of the Continental Divide on vegetation.

Timberline Along the Great Divide

Even the most casual observer cannot help but notice the ecological boundary of timberline — the limit of forests high up on the mountainside. There are actually two timberlines along most of the Divide: lower and upper. Normally, upper timberline is not an abrupt boundary but,

Top: *Timber-covered hills sweep up to a dividing ridge well above timberline in Highland Mountains south of Butte.* RON GLOVAN Left: *Alpine conditions caused by high winds are seen on Lewis and Clark Pass, looking to the north.* BILL CUNNINGHAM Right: *As the Divide enters Moose Creek Plateau of Yellowstone National Park, much tree cover consists of mature lodgepole pine.* GEORGE WUERTHNER

rather, a gradual transition zone between continuous forest below and treeless alpine tundra above.

In most of the mountainous forests of the Continental Divide the elevational ranges of tree species overlap like roof shingles. The drought-resistent species that form the lower timberline give way through a series of transitions to cold-tolerant species near the upper timberline. However, in the extremely dry Continental Divide country of Montana's southwestern corner only a few species of drought-tolerant trees can survive, and then only within narrow elevational bands. In such cases, two separate forest belts occur, each with its own lower and upper timberlines.

Let us hike up a mountain slope toward the Great Divide. Soon we have reached the upper limit of continuous forest and we find that the trees have become stunted and finally reduced to dwarves. We are standing at the exact upper limit of shrublike trees or "krummholz" (German for "crooked wood"). Our climb toward the Divide through the forest has shown us that the forest line is not always distinct. Instead, we've seen a gradient of increasing tree deformity upslope, so that the positions of forest line and krummholz line are imprecise.

Timberline results from many causes, the two most important being climate and topography. At alpine timberlines along the Divide the regional climate is influenced by the local high mountain topography. Other things being equal (which is never the case), we would experience temperatures averaging 3½ degrees F. cooler with each 1,000-foot gain in elevation during our climb. This is known as the lapse rate, or rate of temperature change with increasing elevation. Therefore, if our particular destination on the Divide had been high enough we would have reached a point where the local climate is too cold, snowy, wind-exposed or otherwise severe for trees to survive.

Most of the coniferous tree species along the higher, more rugged portions of Montana's Divide have evolved with considerable hardiness to harsh climates. In general, the regional climates along the Divide in Montana are either maritime or continental.

Maritime timberlines along the Divide are best represented in Glacier Park. These areas are inundated with heavy winter snows and have a cool, cloudy climate year-round. Only during summer is there a period of relative drought.

By contrast, continental climates occur along the crest and eastern slopes of the Divide throughout most of Montana. These climates are characterized by colder, drier conditions, which are often accompanied by heavy winds.

Above: *Thousands of acres of tundra plateau above timberline straddle the Continental Divide as it winds through the massive Scapegoat Mountain complex.*
Below: *"Wind-trained" whitebark pine trees atop the Continental Divide south of Granite Butte show the pruning effect of violent gusts of wind.*
BILL CUNNINGHAM PHOTOS

The topography atop and along the Continental Divide in Montana is every bit as varied and changeable as the weather. In the northern latitudes of Montana, steep south-facing slopes along the Divide receive much more sun than north-facing aspects. This effect becomes more and more evident as one travels north along the Divide, because the sun is limited to an increasingly low, southerly position in the sky. As a result, alpine timberlines along the Divide usually climb higher on southern slopes. The greatest heating occurs in the afternoon when the sun is in a southwesterly position. Thus, southwestern slopes tend to soak up the greatest warmth, with northwestern to eastern aspects being the coolest. Of course, exposures to the southeast to west are relatively warmer.

There are often startling contrasts in trees and undergrowth between adjacent warm and cool exposures. For example, at one point along the Divide in the

Anaconda-Pintler Wilderness I've seen pure stands of whitebark pine with almost no understory on a southwestern slope a few yards away from the sharp crest of the Divide where a lush stand of subalpine larch and heath occupy a cool aspect.

In the mountains of Montana prevailing winds blow from the west and southwest. These winds raise much of the snow off windward slopes and drop it on the leeward side. This pattern reinforces the warmth and dryness of western and southern slopes and causes the opposite east- and north-facing slopes to be even more cool and moist. Again, there are plenty of dry, windy stretches along the Divide where the windward slopes are constantly swept free of snow. The resulting lack of snow insulation prevents trees from getting started, thus lowering the upper timberline.

The undulating and constantly changing topography along the Great Divide consists largely of a series of convex ridges and adjacent concave draws or basins. Usually, convex surfaces are warmer than concave sites. Cold air will settle in the heads of valleys so that summer frost is a common occurrence, while the nearby ridges remain frost-free. I've experienced many chilly mornings in high Continental Divide basins where the temperature was at least 20 degrees colder than on the dividing ridge higher up. This pattern of cold-air ponding often allows trees to grow at much higher elevations on the slopes or ridges of the Divide than in the lower basins or "cirques" (cup-shaped glacial basins frequently found along the headwalls of the Divide). In effect, the timberline is "inverted" with tree-covered ridges towering above alpine tundra at the heads of valleys.

Factors of Influence on the Timberline

It may be that temperature is the single greatest factor influencing the boundary of timberline along the Divide. More than anything else, lack of heat limits the elevation to which trees can ascend. While hardy conifers certainly can survive periods of bitter cold — 60 degrees F. below zero and beyond — they still need a growing season of about two months with nothing more severe than an occasional light frost. Thus, a certain amount of heat is essential if these high altitude trees are to complete their annual growth cycle. Very likely, some of the less hardy species in the subalpine forest along the Divide cannot reach timberline because of a periodic hard frost in early to late summer.

The alpine limits of timberline along the Divide seem to correlate roughly with the location of the 50 degrees isotherm (line on a map connecting spots where a particular temperature occurs) for the warmest month, which is July along Montana's Continental Divide. Portions of the Divide where the mean July temperature is colder than 50 degrees are normally beyond timberline. Most timberline conifers are very frost-hardy during fall, winter and spring. However, by midsummer they've become frost-sensitive and their new needles and shoots can be damaged by temperatures as mild as 27 degrees, depending on the species.

Another frequent occurrence atop the Great Divide is the violent wind, with gusts of hurricane proportions, that can hit during any season on the exposed ridges and peaks. Winds are probably the major cause of dwarfing and krummholz formation at most of the Continental Divide timberlines. A close examination of the upper timberline along the Divide almost certainly will reveal mechanical wind damage to the branches and crowns of trees. Usually, a hurricane-force wind of 60 to 100 m.p.h. is needed to inflict that kind of injury.

In addition warm, dry chinook winds help cause a condition called "winter drought," which literally dries out the foliage. Many striking examples of winter drought, also called red belt, can be found along Montana's Divide. This condition is most pronounced at lower timberline along and east of the Divide. The sudden chinook winds with the accompanying warm, dry air cause death or severe defoliation of trees at the same time that their frozen roots are unable to replace the lost moisture. Normally, the harsh drying that results in red-belt damage is localized to bands on the lower to mid-elevation slopes. Red belt seems to attack stands of ponderosa pine, lodgepole pine and Douglas fir, but limber pine along the lower timberline is unaffected.

On wind-exposed stretches of the Divide, prevailing summer winds from the west at least partially may cause "wind-trained" trees at the upper timberline. Violent gusts of wind, often accompanied by sleet and ice, literally prune the growth off the windward side of trees. There are areas scattered along the crest of the southern Bitterroot Range where the entire timberline zone consists of wind-pruned trees, varying from drawfs at timberline to patches of cushion krummholz less than 12 inches high in the lee side of rocks at the edge of tundra.

There are several relatively low mountain passes along the Divide, well below normal timberline, that are so lashed by wind that they support only stunted and even krummholz trees. The passes funnel and concentrate the wind to amazing velocities. Interestingly, these wind-depressed timberlines often contain species such as lodgepole pine, quaking aspen and Douglas fir not found at true alpine timberlines.

During winter, winds hitting the Divide move snow from exposed to sheltered slopes. In so doing, snow protection and soil moisture are removed from the windward slopes which, in turn, harms tree growth. Many of the exposed, rounded slopes of the Divide never retain enough snowpack to support trees. This causes the phenomenon of ridgetop grasslands, or "balds," surrounded by heavy forests on the less exposed slopes at lower elevations.

Snowpack along the Divide helps trees by protecting them from the extremes of cold, freezing, thawing and drying wind. The krummholz community is a good example of extremely hardy vegetation that depends on snowpack to safeguard it from drying and from mechanical injury in winter.

Avalanche is yet another factor that locally influences the location of timberline. Snow slides scar, flatten and break tree trunks on many Continental Divide slopes, lowering timberlines in large basins. The upper slopes of the Divide are well marked with the signatures of past avalanches that literally mowed down vertical swathes of forest along the valley walls.

Probably the major effect of heavy snows along Divide timberlines is to prevent trees from growing in otherwise suitable sites. At many places in the high country snow covers the ground until mid- to late summer, so that the already short growing season is too short to support tree growth. Conifers are limited to the tops of humps in snowy basins where the snowpack is comparatively thin in some places along the western slopes of the Divide in Glacier Park.

That snowfall can be augmented by wind is well illustrated in the deep cirque basin of the Grinnell Glacier in Glacier Park. Here, a precipitation gauge below the glacier at the mid-range elevation of 6,113 feet (well below the usual timberline elevation) collects an average of 147 inches of precipitation annually, even though the adjacent mountain country gets about 60 inches.

Of course, winter snowpack recharges the soil water source, supplying water for plant roots. This snowpack is the only dependable water supply for much of the semi-arid Divide country. Thus, the occurrence of forest often coincides with the areas containing snowpack, partly because winds dump more snow in the timber than in the open alpine tundra and grasslands. Also, the forest shades the snowpack, thereby slowing the melt.

Along many of the eastern slopes and southwestern stretches of the Divide precipitation is simply too infrequent to support forests. This dry pattern is largely responsible for the formation of lower timberlines. On the other hand, because of the factors discussed above, inadequate precipitation seldom limits the upper advance of forest trees. However, low precipitation and the resultant soil drought have a lot to do with which species exist in the timberline stands.

The critical level of precipitation needed for forest growth varies with temperature, type of soil or geology, and the seasonal distribution of the moisture itself. An example of these intertwined effects may be seen in the high, semi-arid valleys below Montana's Divide. Here, enough precipitation to support the most drought-resistant trees, such as ponderosa pine, may occur only at elevations above 7,000 feet where the growing season is too short for our beautiful state tree.

Along some of the drier reaches of the Great Divide, thick forests of lodgepole pine and subalpine fir change abruptly along a nearly straight-line boundary to luxuriant grass-forb communities amid scattered Douglas fir trees. These distinct lines of vegetation usually coincide with changes in the geologic substrate. The dense forest is growing on acidic rocks, such as granite, argillite or shale, while the herbfields with open-grown dry-site trees arise from adjacent limestone. Much of the limestone weathers to a coarse, droughty soil. Soil scientists have learned that although growing sites on granitic soils can support lodgepole pine on 16 inches or more of annual precipitation, similar sites on limestone need nearly twice as much moisture for lodgepole to survive. Hence, we encounter the profound vegetative boundaries described above along the drier, eastern slopes of the Divide whereas some of the wetter western slopes support similar plant communities on adjoining acid rock and limestone.

It is also possible that lack of viable seed may cause the formation of upper timberline along some of the Divide since stunted trees, especially krummholz, rarely produce much of a seed crop. Higher elevation timberline along segments of the Divide may result from conditions that are too tough for seed production, rather than from conditions that are too harsh for tree growth. Seeds need to be transported only about one-half mile along most of the Divide in order to spread from timberline trees to alpine tundra. Strong upslope winds along most of the Divide provide for this type of seed dispersal.

Without question, major natural disturbances impact the level of timberline. We've already discussed the effects of avalanches in steep Divide areas that get heavy snowfall. In areas of Glacier Park avalanches are so frequent and devastating that they prevent what would otherwise be a sub-alpine forest on the landscape. Instead, these avalanche strips are occupied by a rich mosaic of plant communities, including small, injured conifers and resilient shrubs, such as alder. Even these avalanche-prone areas support patches of forest on the convex spur ridges and intervening moderate slopes.

Fire is another disturbance that can lower upper timberline or raise the lower timberline. In general, the past half-century or more of fire suppression by the Forest Service and other agencies has not affected alpine timberline forests as much as the general forest zone at lower elevations. This is because the normally sparse, broken fuels and cool, moist conditions at alpine timberlines along the Divide usually prevent large, destructive fires regardless of the level of fire suppression. However, the common occurrence of lightning strikes and high winds along the Divide causes many fires to ignite and a few of them to spread, particularly along the exposed ridges. Occasionally a large fire from below spreads into a timberline forest, but more often timberline fires burn only a few tree clumps or isolated trees.

Before the days of intensive fire suppression, fires were usually frequent and small, passing underneath open-growing trees at lower timberline, killing a few of them. The less frequent severe fire often would allow grasslands or shrubs to take over the site because of the slowness of tree regeneration. Now, as a result of fire suppression and heavy livestock grazing, lower timberlines have either crept downslope or become thicker.

Biological factors, such as insects and disease, can cause severe damage to timberline trees, but are usually not important in determining the location of timberline itself. Extensive forests of mature whitebark pine along the timberlines of the Divide were killed by mountain pine beetles between 1909 and 1940. The larvae of this indigenous insect spend the winter in the inner bark, tunneling around the circumference of the trunk while busily feeding. The result is girdling and killing of the tree. Interestingly, only the large, vigorous trees have an inner bark thick enough to attract the tiny predators. Thus, the younger trees are spared. In the late 1970s new outbreaks of the beetle killed most of the whitebark pine along and near the western slopes of the Divide in Glacier Park. In these moist, northwestern reaches of Montana's Continental Divide the combined effects of blister rust infection, mountain pine beetles and fire suppression are changing the composition of timberline forests.

Western larch, a deciduous conifer that blazes yellow in the fall, is abundant in the general forest zone along west slopes of the Divide in Inland Maritime climatic zone. JEFF GNASS

Animal "tree planters" also put their mark on the timberline. Certain jays harvest and cache huge quantities of seed from ponderosa, limber and whitebark pines, particularly near the upper and lower timberlines. The berrylike cones of junipers, which grow at lower timberline, are randomly seeded across the land by various birds that consume them. The seeds of junipers do not easily germinate unless their fleshy coatings are dissolved by passing through the digestive systems of birds or other animals. Without question, "nature's tree planters" spread seeds over a larger area than would otherwise occur, but again, they have little influence on the position of timberline.

The hardy trees of Montana's alpine Divide country represent the response of trees to increasingly severe environmental conditions. One can only marvel at the tenacity of a struggling krummholz spruce, perhaps centuries old and less than a foot in height, as it ekes out a living from a rocky, windblown perch almost devoid of soil, warmth, usable moisture and shelter.

Forest Patterns

In general, the northern and western portions of Montana's Continental Divide are wetter because of the strong oceanic influence on their climate. Much of this Divide country is covered by a dense mantle of continuous forest, with several of the Pacific maritime trees represented. Usually, only the highest peaks that rise above 7,000 feet develop any kind of alpine timberline.

As would be expected, the southern and eastern sections of Montana's Divide have drier, more continental climates. Pacific tree and undergrowth species are absent. The forests tend to be broken and are often limited to cool, moist exposures and higher elevations. The most extensive vegetation consists of sagebrush and grasslands. Drought-caused timberlines at lower altitudes are common. Here the Divide tends to be higher than that farther north, ranging from 9,000 feet to over 11,000 feet. Alpine timberlines are found along most of the southern portion of the Divide, along with small patches of tundra.

To provide a glimpse of broad vegetative patterns along the Divide we can separate the country into four major climatic regions — inland maritime, northern continental, intermountain and southern continental.

Inland Maritime

The best examples of upper timberline country along the Divide in the inland maritime zone are the western Continental Divide slopes of Glacier Park. Pacific air masses in the winter cause milder temperatures than in the other zones. Trees at higher elevations are solidly encased in a "snow cocoon" most of the winter and so are not subjected to drying. I have observed some of the maritime species such as western hemlock growing almost to the Continental Divide above Lake MacDonald in Glacier Park. Here the forest growth is noticeably denser. The upper timberlines along this northwestern stretch of the Divide receive an average of 60 to 70 inches of annual precipitation, with some of the high cirque basins getting more than 100 inches.

Even in this climatic zone subzero continental polar air occasionally invades during the winter. The harshness of conditions along the Divide in Glacier is evident at Logan Pass (6,664 feet) on the Going-to-the-Sun Highway. Tree line rises to only 7,000 feet. Ribbon forest and snow-glade formations of mostly subalpine fir can be observed at Logan Pass and on the way to the Hidden Lake Overlook. Extensive snowfields normally remain until early August. Even in midsummer, storms sometimes dump a foot or more of fresh, wet snow. Hurricane-force winds commonly blast forth severe blizzards when Pacific and continental air masses collide along this rugged spine of the Continental Divide. The summer dry season is fleeting and intermittent. Only stunted subalpine fir, dwarf Engelmann spruce and whitebark pine are left scattered throughout lush meadows filled with bright yellow glacier lilies.

An uprooted whitebark pine atop the Divide just north of Lewis and Clark Pass gives mute evidence of the awesome tree-shaping force of the wind as it picks up momentum through this natural tunnel. BILL CUNNINGHAM

Northern Continental

The northern continental climatic zone extends roughly along the eastern slopes of the Divide from the 49th Parallel to the Helena area. The climate is a bit more moist than farther south, resulting in lower timberlines at 4,000 to 5,000 feet. This is the northern "chinook belt" where the extension of the continental polar air mass from northern Canada mixes with the influx of mild Pacific air during much of the winter. Ponderosa pine is unable to grow along these east side slopes because of severe red belt conditions caused by rapid changes in temperature with high winds.

Along this segment of the Divide the lower slopes are covered with lodgepole pine and Douglas fir. At higher elevations the forest changes to subalpine fir, Engelmann spruce and whitebark pine. Upper timberline lowers to about 7,500 feet along the eastern slopes of the Divide in Glacier Park, climbing to over 8,000 feet at the latitude of Helena farther south.

Prevailing winds of 30 miles per hour or more are common along the northeastern slopes of the Divide. A dramatic example of wind-modified trees occurs at the moderate elevation of Lewis and Clark Pass (6,400 feet), a Continental Divide Pass accessible via a short hike from the gravel road up Alice Creek northeast of Lincoln. This historic pass, traveled by Captain Lewis on his return trip in 1806, is a truly spectacular wind tunnel. The pass contains numerous alpine tundra species, even though it is 2,000 feet below the normal lower limits of tundra. These cushion-like plants grow in patches between krummholz shapes of mid-elevation Douglas fir and aspen and subalpine whitebark pine and Engelmann spruce.

Along the high Divide ridges of the Bob Marshall Wilderness grow small patches of stunted alpine larch. These trees are found on north-facing slopes and cirques at upper timberline, but are absent on dry, limestone soils.

Intermountain

The intermountain portion of the Divide has more of an "intermediate" climate. Although it is heavily influenced by Pacific air masses, it does not receive the deluge of snow, rain and cloud cover common to the inland maritime climate farther north. The forests of ponderosa pine, Douglas fir and western larch (west of the Divide) often begin as low as 4,000 feet, giving way to whitebark pine and subalpine fir up to 9,000 feet.

Alpine timberlines are extensive in several of the intermountain ranges, such as the Anaconda-Pintlers. There are impressive, open stands of gigantic whitebark pine with widely-spreading branches on the Divide ridge and on some of the nearby gentle south-facing slopes in this region. Beautiful timberline parklands of subalpine fir, Engelmann spruce, alpine larch, with luxuriant growths of grouse whortleberry and red mountain heath occur in moist cirque basins and northern exposures. Most of these timberlines were glaciated and therefore have extensive amounts of exposed rock, cliffs and talus.

Pure, open stands of alpine larch cover many of the northern-aspect talus slopes along this portion of the Divide. Such sites are normally treeless in mountains lacking alpine larch. These glorious trees can be identified readily from great distances when they turn a brilliant gold in late September. Glacial moraines and avalanche chutes in the highest cirques of the Divide are often dominated by alpine larch. Despite the obvious hardiness of this species, it apparently is unable to compete for growing space with other conifers downslope.

Here, south-facing slopes at upper timberline are dominated by whitebark pine. Many of these stands have been turned into eerie ghostlike forms of sun-bleached snags as a result of mountain pine beetle epidemics in the early 1900s. The smaller whitebark pines that escaped the beetle continue to dominate these sites, even when next to more shade-tolerant subalpine fir. It seems that the fir is less hardy in these open, cold-dry stretches of the Divide.

Continued on Page 37

Weather Station Records

From selected lower elevation forested sites in each of Montana's Continental Divide Forest Regions.

Region and Station	Elev.	Mean mo. temp. Jan.	Mean mo. temp. July	avg. frost-free season	mean an. precpt.	mean an. snowfall
Northwestern Polebridge	3,690'	17F.	61F.	30 days	23"	122"
West-Central Darby	3,815'	25F.	65F.	99 days	16"	60"
North-Central Babb	4,300'	19F.	60F.	60 days	20"	93"
Central Helena	3,893'	19F.	68F.	134 days	11"	48"
Southwestern Lakeview	6,710'	10F.	59F.	30 days	20"	142"
South-Central W. Yellowstone	6,662'	12F.	60F.	30 days	21"	145"

Left top: *Framed by whitebark and lodgepole pines atop the Divide at the head of the Little Blackfoot River, Cottonwood Lake breaks up a continuous treescape in the Intermountain climatic zone.*
Left bottom: *A pasque flower graces the Divide just south of Priest Pass.*
Above: *Alpine conditions can be created by violent winds at unusually low elevation such as here at Lewis and Clark Pass.*
BILL CUNNINGHAM PHOTOS

Purely Natural—
Research Natural
Areas on the Divide

Much of Montana's Great Divide remains wild, free and natural. Still, even the wildest and most remote stretches have been modified to some extent by human activities. At times the effects of these activities are subtle, like fire suppression. At other times the changes are as dramatic and noticeable as a 500KV transmission line near Champion Pass or an open pit phosphate mine atop the crest of the Centennials. But a few priceless remnants of unmodified plant communities survive along the Divide. These areas are classified as research natural areas (RNA's) by the Forest Service and other resource agencies.

Research natural areas are established for observation, study and nonmanipulative research. It is hoped that the several proposed RNA's represent a wide range of pristine forest, grassland, alpine and geological landscapes along or near our nation's backbone in Montana. In addition to research and study, the protection of natural areas can preserve genetic diversity, safeguard against serious environmental changes, allow them to serve as baselines for studying plant succession and long-term ecological changes, provide educational activities and act as control areas to monitor the impacts of development in similar types of environments.

Ideally, a designated natural area should encompass an entire small drainage that shows no evidence of major human-caused disturbances. The Forest Service and other agencies protect natural areas against land uses that would modify natural ecological processes, such as logging and livestock grazing. Most recreational uses are generally compatible with the natural world and would be regulated only if harmful to the primary research and educational purposes of an RNA. To add yet another layer of protection, the Forest Service and the Bureau of Land Management normally would withdraw a natural area from mining and mineral entry.

Following are short descriptions of several potential RNA's and other protected areas atop or close to the Continental Divide in Montana. Each of these areas has been inventoried and surveyed on the ground for its natural ecological value, but thus far only Cliff Lake and Red Rocks have been formally designated as "natural areas." The remaining areas are proposed as RNA's in the respective Forestwide Plans released by the Forest Service during 1985.

These areas are not the only examples of their representative natural communities, nor are they necessarily the best ones. But they are available here and now for natural-area purposes if we have the foresight to preserve them.

From north to south, and in most cases on national forest land, we find the following.

A brass cap marks the top of the Continental Divide and 8,597' Thunderbolt Mountain between Helena and Butte. BILL CUNNINGHAM

1. **Granite Butte** — 480 acres — just south of Stemple Pass on the Helena National Forest. This area, which straddles the Divide, is a mountain grassland surrounded by subalpine forests of Englemann spruce, subalpine fir, whitebark pine and lodgepole pine. Snow patterns along the Divide have formed a whitebark pine ribbon forest and nearby snow glades of wet sedges and rushes. Very little of this country has escaped livestock grazing. At one time the beautiful fescue meadows of Granite Butte were grazed heavily by sheep, causing a marked reduction in native forbs. The site has been closed to grazing for the past 15 years and is better for natural area purposes than any other nearby area. However, its integrity may be threatened by off-road vehicles, trespass grazing and mining.

2. **Thunderbolt Mountain** — 500 acres — Deerlodge National Forest between Helena and Butte. This is a wet area derived from granitic and volcanic substrates, which includes seeps and edges of lush meadows immediately east of one of the highest central Montana Continental Divide peaks — 8,597' Thunderbolt Mountain. The upland forest of this proposed RNA is dominated by mature lodgepole pine (more than 100 years old). The area is next to extensive clearcuts and, as such, would be a good baseline area for comparative monitoring.

3. **Bernice** — 450 acres — Deerlodge National Forest on the Boulder River a few miles south of Thunderbolt Mountain. This small but significant watershed is characterized by aspen stands, a permanent pond and bunchgrass meadows.

4. **Basin Creek** — 800 acres — Deerlodge Forest. The Great Divide forms the western boundary of this portion of the Basin Creek municipal watershed in the Highland Mountains south of Butte. The trees are mostly lodgepole pine and Engelmann spruce with a few pockets of aspen and only one small patch of subalpine fir. The gentle Basin Creek and connected wetlands flow through the area providing alder and willow thickets which, in turn, account for extensive use by moose and beaver.

5. **Goat Flats** — 400 acres — Deerlodge Forest. This is a spectacular high alpine stretch of the Divide deep inside the Anaconda-Pintler Wilderness. This lofty plateau supports extensive alpine turf and cushion plant communities in addition to a number of rare plants.

6. **Dexter Basin** — 900 acres — Deerlodge Forest along the northern end of the Anaconda-Pintler Wilderness. A key aspect of Dexter Basin is the series of permanent ponds below the high cirque wall to the south. Although the ponds seem to be devoid of fish, the abundance of big freshwater shrimp attests to a varied invertebrate population, common when predation by fish is lacking. Avalanche chutes and 140-year-old lodgepole pines occur on the edges of the scenic subalpine basin.

Mountain grasslands surround a windblown ribbon of whitebark pine and Englemann spruce in the proposed Granite Butte Research Natural Area, with the Divide winding from here south through the snow-covered ridges of Nevada Mountain. BILL CUNNINGHAM

7. East Fork Bitterroot — undetermined acreage — Bitterroot Forest just inside the northwestern boundary of the Anaconda-Pintler Wilderness along the East Fork trail. This is a wetlands ecosystem at about 5,600' with numerous beaver ponds edged by several species of willow. On the higher ground is shrubby cinquefoil and bluebunch wheatgrass giving way to an upland conifer forest of lodgepole pine.

8. Red Rock Lakes National Wildlife Refuge — RNA of U.S. Fish & Wildlife Service, 38,144 acres — a wilderness marshland in the heart of the Centennial Valley of southwestern Montana beneath the northern slopes of the Centennial Mountains. With the Divide only 1½ miles to the south, elevations range from 6,600' to 9,600' at Sheep Mountain. There are 14,000 acres of open water and marsh with the remaining lands being wet meadows, bogs, grasslands, subalpine meadows and forests. The expansive upper and lower Red Rock Lakes contain inland saline marsh along their north ends. East of Upper Red Rock Lake are several deep, open freshwater ponds used for brooding and feeding by trumpeter swans. This remarkable complex has a series of undisturbed, high-elevation ecosystem types that give us a glimpse of what the country was like before whites arrived. The ecosystem includes wetlands, upland meadows and forests. Red Rocks is an outstanding waterfowl production area and provides irreplaceable habitat for rare species such as trumpeter swan, peregrine falcon, bald and golden eagles and arctic grayling.

9. Cliff Lake RNA — 2,291 acres — Beaverhead National Forest. This southwest Montana area consists of a high, undulating bench atop ancient volcanics, which rise sharply some 600' above Cliff Lake — a natural impoundment caused by a glacial moraine. The grasslands are rich in the number of range species. The forest consists of 100-year-old lodgepole pine and 200-year-old Douglas fir.

10. Obsidian Sands — 350 acres — Gallatin National Forest, located two miles west of Yellowstone Park, bordering the south arm of Hebgen Lake. This area is representative of the surrounding 100 square miles of obsidian-sand benchlands of alluvial origin. The site is a textbook example of the lodgepole pine/bitterbrush habitat type.

These 10, mostly small, natural areas totaling but a few thousand acres along the slopes of Montana's Continental Divide from near Stemple Pass south to Yellowstone Park are but a few surviving pages in the book of ecological time. They give us a kaleidoscopic glimpse of the effect of natural processes on the land that the once-formidable barrier of the Great Divide served well to protect.

Left top: *Topography and climate conspire to create a scattered subalpine forest with timberline along that portion of the Great Divide that forms the head of Moose Creek in the southern Bitterroots.*

Left bottom: *Aspen and other deciduous plants seek out the wetter gullies as Douglas fir trees fill the spaces between rocks on the drier side slopes just west of Homestake Pass.*

Below: *From the ashes of the 1,300-acre Gibbons Pass fire begins a new cycle of forest succession. This July 1985 wildfire was kindled atop the Continental Divide by a lightning strike. Although both sides of the Divide burned, most of the fire occurred on the east-side Beaverhead National Forest. Fire fighters experienced some tense moments as a downdraft from a fast-moving thunderhead exploded the blaze from one acre to 200 acres almost instantly.*
BILL CUNNINGHAM PHOTOS

Southern Continental

The cool, dry country of the southern continental climatic region encompasses the Continental Divide of southwestern Montana. Sagebrush-grasslands cover the valleys and lower slopes of the Divide and forest is limited to the higher elevations. This stretch of the Divide lies in the rain shadow downwind from central Idaho's high mountain mass and therefore receives very little Pacific storm moisture. Average yearly precipitation is only eight to 14 inches in the high valleys east of the Divide. Lower timberlines often begin at 6,000 to 7,000 feet, consisting of Douglas fir and some limber pine. The country is too cold for ponderosa pine. The narrow forest belt along the Divide will have timberline developing at around 9,300 feet. In fact, south of Dillon in the dry Continental Divide mountains of the Italian Peaks and the Lima Peaks, sagebrush and grasslands extend completely through the subalpine zone. The only timber consists of isolated stringers in north-facing gullies.

The combined effects of fire suppression and livestock grazing have caused a reduction in grass and a substantial invasion of Douglas fir down the eastern slopes of the southwestern corner of Montana's Great Divide. Once open-grown stands of Douglas fir are now much thicker forests. Before the country was settled in the late 1880s, wildfires burned in the lower timberline every 25 to 40 years. Because it takes about 40 years for Douglas fir seedlings to become large enough to withstand fire, they were limited to wet or rocky sites where fire was less frequent. Fire suppression has changed all this so that now the trees are able to survive in these dry forest sites.

Even in this dry climatic region, wet timberline areas occur in high cirque basins below the peaks of the Divide. Here, islands of subalpine fir, Engelmann spruce and whitebark pine are scattered throughout lush, alpine meadows and rocky talus slopes. The best example of this that I've seen is in the West Big Hole country along the Divide west of Jackson.

The high, rounded ridges branching from the Divide in this region often produce huge, spreading whitebark pines with an understory of elk sedge and grouse whortleberry. This vegetative pattern may change suddenly to subalpine grassland as the site becomes a little drier because of a more southerly aspect.

With the peaks of Glacier Park to the north, this broad stretch of the Continental Divide was heavily grazed by domestic sheep during the 1940s. MONTANA HISTORICAL SOCIETY

Human Uses of Montana's Timberline Divide

Humans and domestic animals have caused widespread, often severe damage to upper timberlines throughout most of the world. It has only been during the past decade or two that similar impacts have begun to appear in the Northern Rockies. Montana is part of the Rocky Mountain state region that experienced the fastest rate — some 37 percent — of population growth in the nation during the decade of the 1970s. In turn, this growth has created pressure for increased suburban and rural land subdivisions as more and more people seek to enjoy the amenities of subalpine country living. Land speculation, rural subdivision and development threaten some of the most scenic portions of the lower timberline along the Divide.

Fortunately, a majority of the Continental Divide country in Montana is publicly owned with a management direction that is generally designed to maintain natural vegetative communities. Wilderness designation protects some portions of the Divide along with several research natural areas, national park land and other protective classifications. Still, much of the Divide remains open and vulnerable to a variety of land uses that could adversely affect the fragile alpine timberline country.

Of all the land uses, overgrazing by domestic livestock has the most widespread impact on alpine timberlines along the Divide, although the impact in Montana has been less severe than in Rocky Mountain states to the south. Much of the damage, including accelerated erosion, has been caused by past excessive grazing of domestic sheep at the upper timberline.

A growing demand for dispersed outdoor recreation continues to impact alpine timberlines along Montana's

Top: *The site of the Penobscot Mine as it appears today.* BILL
CUNNINGHAM
Bottom: *Butte in August 1890. The Continental Divide tops the
range of mountains on the horizon at right.* HAYNES FOUND.
COLL., MONTANA HISTORICAL SOCIETY

Above: *Increasingly, fragile alpine timberlines along the Continental Divide are being impacted by recreational uses.* COURTESY, U.S.
FOREST SERVICE
Below: *Located precisely on top of the Continental Divide near Marysville, the Penobscot Mine is only now being reclaimed after
having been abandoned more than a century ago.* MONTANA HISTORICAL SOCIETY

Top: *Tenacious clumps of low-lying vegetation at 9,000-plus feet on the western flanks of Scapegoat Mountain.* BILL CUNNINGHAM
Above: *Well above timberline, the rocky summit of Thunderbolt Mountain touches on a proposed Research Natural Area that may help teach us how better to manage other areas for commodity production.* BILL CUNNINGHAM

The Great Divide in the Anaconda-Pintler Range defines headwalls, convex ridges and snowclad peaks as the ever-changing phenomenon of timberline dances to the rhythm of wind, topography and climate. RON GLOVAN

Divide. Resulting abuses run the gamut from mindless hacking down of live trees for firewood to the proposed development of massive destination ski resorts and second-home condominium tracts.

Portions of Montana's Continental Divide country have been scoured and picked over for nearly 120 years by optimistic miners certain of discovering the "mother lode." However, high-technology mineral and oil and gas exploration at alpine timberlines poses a whole new set of potential impacts that could go far beyond anything we've yet seen. The disturbances of mining, drilling pads, pipelines, construction sites, work camps, extensive networks of new roads and all of the associated human uses could be extremely disruptive at upper timberlines near the crest of the Divide. Large areas of similar disturbances already have occurred in parts of the high Absaroka and Beartooth Ranges. Reclamation specialists have found it hard to achieve even minimal revegetation.

Despite these problems, impacts and issues, more and more people are recognizing the vital importance of the alpine timberlines of the Divide as a source of high-quality water for municipal and agricultural uses. The high basins and lofty ridges of the Great Divide provide year-round snowpack and water storage. In addition, the upper timberlines are biologically rich ecotones (transitions between varied vegetative communities) that have immeasurable value as banks of species and genetic diversity.

There is a parallel between the incredibly hardy, tenacious plants that cling to life in the harsh environment of the Great Divide and the increasing need in our controlled, sanitized society to experience the raw, primeval forces of nature that are so magnificently represented by Northern Rockies Continental Divide country at timberline. Thankfully, we're not yet able to control these forces.

Denizens
of the Great Divide

After setting up camp in Halfmoon Park north of massive Scapegoat Mountain, I took a solo hike across the headwaters of the Dearborn River, climbing the nearly vertical east wall of Scapegoat up a couloir. As I scrambled near the top of the wall I found myself almost eyeball to eyeball with a large male mountain goat resting on a rock ledge. The late afternoon sunlight filtered through his sleek white coat as he bolted over the top to the Pacific side of the Divide. Reaching the southeast summit of Scapegoat (8,803'), I spotted two golden eagles perched on a rock directly atop the Great Divide about one-half mile to the north. Images of these powerful predators swooping down and knocking young goats off sheer cliffs came to mind as I reflected upon the significance of seeing both a mountain goat and one of his few natural predators in such close proximity. As I glassed the subalpine basins to the south, I was treated to the sight of two bull elk feeding on the green grass in preparation for the stress of the rut and the oncoming winter. I knew that the mature bull and his younger companion were there because of the security and good-quality forage provided by this remote segment of the Divide. Dropping back into the upper Dearborn River basin, I jumped two large mule deer bucks in a boulder field at the foot of the limestone face of the Great Divide. They stopped and looked back every so often out of curiosity, giving me the chance to enjoy their agile beauty in the shadow of the awesome Scapegoat massif.

Impressions, values, images, relationships between wildlife and the wildness evoked by that undisturbed stretch of the Divide produced in me a sense of genuine awe.

The west slope cutthroat trout, Montana's state fish and practically the state's only native trout species, inhabits tiny streams only a stone's throw from the Continental Divide where they have been protected by waterfalls and logjams from hybridization downstream. Their survival is insured only by maintenance of very high quality, undisturbed watershed. ED WOLFF

As Montana was being settled, homesteaders swarmed westward like locusts across the prairies. Although they founded an agrarian society, their subsistence living required wildlife as a source of food. Wildlife populations were severely depleted with little thought of the future. Man exploited the more fertile lands first, leaving the rugged, inhospitable Divide for last. This very inhospitality caused most of Montana's Divide country to remain in the public domain, and not to be homesteaded or otherwise converted into private ownership.

The description of wildlife habitat along the Divide as "prime" is relative, because we've already converted the most fertile land to non-wildlife uses. The remote, rugged high country of most of Montana's Divide is among the last places in the state to be exploited. Therefore, these areas are among the best places for certain species that need security from human activities, such as mountain goats, mountain sheep, grizzly bears, elk, big old mule deer bucks, whitetailed ptarmigan, harlequin ducks, hoary marmots and pikas. They need to be free from competing with humans for the land.

When you view mountain goats picking their way along the face of the Chinese Wall, or elk migrating across Sun River Pass, you're looking at something genuine — "museum pieces" that have evolved and remained in their native wild habitats along the Continental Divide. When wildlife was being decimated in more accessible areas, many species did make their last stands along the Divide; their descendants live there today. It was a time when wildlife's only survival option was the remote isolation of Great Divide wilderness, where they waited for us to regain our senses. Now, generations later, we have allowed wildlife to recover in many places through sound conservation practices.

Except for mountain goats, we've decreased the available habitat and increased the hunter harvest of all of Montana's ungulate species. Even though we've eliminated elk from the more fertile land, hunter harvest has gone up as a result of improved wildlife management, acquisition of key winter ranges, and enforcement of game laws. Traditional goat habitat has been left mostly intact because no one has figured out a reason or way to exploit the highest, most remote reaches of the Continental Divide.

Mountain Goats

Mountain goats are the best indicator species of Montana's Divide. This lofty crest is the easternmost extension of native goat habitat. The high, harsh, craggy nature of much of the Divide is precisely the environmental niche that suits the mountain goat. When you see goats along the rugged backbone of Glacier or the Bob Marshall you are seeing the real thing — an authentic native population that has evolved for tens of thousands of years in that habitat. These are not descendants of a transplanted population.

The mountain goat is a breed apart — the only genus and species of its kind in the world. Goats have evolved to become incredible specialists, perfectly adapted to a narrow, harsh environment along the rugged crest of the Continent. The body of the goat represents this remarkable adaptation: low center of gravity; short, powerful legs built for pulling power rather than speed; spongy, thick tissue on the bottom of the hooves with a foot that spreads out for superior grip on rocks; more prominent dew claws for better mobility in deep snow. Still, goats probably have the highest natural mortality of any North American ungulate. Avalanches and falls from cliffs take their toll.

Despite the dangers, goats need the kind of cliff country typified by much of the Divide to survive. They make considerable use of forests and other environments, but the security of remote crags, peaks and ridges must be close at hand.

Because of their specialization, goats typify the Divide more than any other native species. Other animals, such as elk and deer, are generalists that inhabit a wide variety of habitats from riparian lowlands to the alpine crest of the Divide.

Hunting is important to the survival of goat populations as a means of maintaining public interest and support for the species. However, hunter harvest levels must be extremely conservative. Only two to 10 percent of the population can be harvested as opposed to around 25 percent of elk and deer. This is because goats respond less readily to reduced population levels by increasing their reproductive rate.

Weather influences goats' behavior and population more profoundly than it does any other mountain animal. Environmental conditions in goat country are more predictable because of its high, barren nature. These rocky areas are less affected by wildfires and other vegetative changes than is the lower forest zone. This severe but relatively stable environment contributes to the traditional nature of the beast.

Continental Divide goat habitat, both summer and winter, is one and the same. Even so, the winter migrations of some males have been tracked from the head of the Flathead River over the Divide east to the rocky reefs of the Rocky Mountain Front overlooking the prairie — an area of some 30 square miles. The windswept slopes of the Divide are among the few places where goats, especially nannies and kids, often move *upward* in winter to search for forage.

Alpine ranges along the Divide during winter offer goats a nutrition advantage over grazing areas at lower elevations. Mountain goats select winter diets in the alpine that are nearly twice as digestible as winter diets of mountain sheep, elk and mule deer foraging on lower ranges. Although goats eat almost any plant, they seem to select Douglas-fir needles during winter. They also consume a great deal of moss, which is low in nutritional value but completely digestible. Goats are quite selective about which parts of the plants they eat, choosing the most digestible portions.

Because of their habitual patterns, goats are extremely vulnerable. They cannot resist salt and will stand still on high ledges licking mineralized soil and rock, thereby making easy targets for hunters. Their outwardly calm disposition is an adaptation to prevent abrupt moves or panic on the exposed pinnacles and ridges where they live. These tenacious mountaineers also will stay in the same area even when their habitat is rendered insecure or

unsuitable because of access roads or other development. The presence of roads has been linked to declines of mountain goat populations across their range in North America.

The goat's home along the Divide is so harsh that kid and yearling survival may be less than 50 percent, depending on the severity of winter. Golden eagles have been known to swoop down and knock young goats off ledges. The young goats' protective reaction is to seek shelter directly under their mothers.

Goats tend to associate in small family groups in order to minimize the effects of accidents in their dangerous, craggy domain. However, large bands of goats are sometimes observed, as illustrated by an account of some 60 years ago in what is now the Anaconda-Pintler Wilderness. Early-day Forest Ranger H.R. Richards wrote:

"On the Continental Divide at the head of the East Fork of Rock Creek is a flat. I rode up to this flat looking for a sheep driveway from the Deerlodge ... I saw a lot of tracks and what I thought was wool on the ground and wondered if sheep had been there ... Right in front of me, instead of sheep, I saw a herd of mountain goats cooling themselves lying on a large bank drift of snow which hung on the side of the cliff. By the number of kids in the herd and the wool and tracks, I believed this flat must be a kidding ground. The goats were frantic because those on the snow bank had no place to go except toward me. There was one nanny that made a break for it with her kid and yearling past me and my horse. I could hardly believe what I was seeing. She went with her offspring down the cliff on the opposite side from where she had been sunning herself with the herd on the snow. She went almost straight down for perhaps 1,000 or 1,500 feet, circled a small lake, then came back up the way I came up, passed on the other side of me, and went up the ridge above the plateau. In the meantime, the other goats finally decided to get going. They dashed off their snow bed right and left and scattered all over. There were at least 25 or more counting the kids. There were also some on either side of me on the ridge."

The adaptation of the mountain goat to living year-round in some of Montana's most austere terrain dramatizes this creature's amazing will to survive. But avalanches, cliff falls and golden eagles pale in comparison to the damage to entire populations that could occur if additional roads and resource development penetrate remote mountain goat country along the Divide.

Bighorn Sheep

Bighorn sheep are often confused with mountain goats. However, anyone who has ever seen the massive, curling horns of a mature ram would never mistake these blocky animals for anything else. Their magnificent horns can weigh up to 30 pounds, or one-tenth of their body weight.

Unlike goats, bighorns are herd animals. They follow age-old migration routes and even use traditional bedding grounds on their way between seasonal ranges. The large rams spend much of their time in high rocky places away from the ewes, lambs and young rams. One of nature's most exciting spectacles is the fierce struggle for supremacy between rams at the onset of mating in late fall.

There is not much overlap between the native ranges of sheep and goats, unless human activities force sheep upward into goat habitat along the Divide. When this happens, both species suffer because they tend to use similar forage. During summer, the cumulative effects on both sheep and goats from competition with livestock grazing, energy exploration and recreation uses can be more severe than those of winter nutrition stress.

If competition can be limited between human uses of the land and these highly social creatures of habit, bighorns will continue to grace Montana's mountains close to the Great Divide.

Elk

A key feature of the Divide is that it provides high-quality vegetative habitat late in the summer grazing season when other browse has dried out below. The high, lush basins below the rocky spine of the Divide are among the last places to turn green and they retain this lushness for the longest period. Here the physical characteristics of the Divide directly influence vegetative patterns, which, in turn, influence animal use. This use is perhaps best represented by the migratory elk — Montana's most prized trophy animal.

The Divide can be thought of as part of an overall wildlife habitat in which various wildlife species attempt to fill each available habitat niche — the way of life unique to each species. Elk have the objective of gaining weight during the

Top: *Bigborn sheep and high country are virtually synonymous.* SHELBA HAMMOND Bottom: *And in the fall, mountains along the Divide resound with the peals from ram battles.* KEN WHITE Right: *Bugling bull elk.* GARY HOLMES

Elk calf. TOM ULRICH

Band of elk on Castle Reef, 1936. Although Castle Reef is not on the Divide, these animals would have been part of the Sun River herd, whose migrations frequently take them across the Divide. COURTESY, U.S. FOREST SERVICE

summer grazing season so as to be ready for the rigors of rut and survival during winter. They are constantly balancing their need for security and their need for weight gain. Bulls don't need to care for calves, so they tend to range more widely in rugged country along the Divide during summer. Their willingness to sacrifice security to put on more weight may explain why most of the elk I saw during summer photo expeditions along the Divide were small groups of males.

Like bighorn sheep, elk are highly social. However, mountain animals in general tend to be more solitary, darker and smaller than their plains counterparts.

A summer-fattened, mature six- to seven-year-old bull weighs from 700 to 1,000 pounds. In September, at the start of the rut, bugling announces the bull's presence and is one of the most thrilling sounds to be heard in the wild

headwater basins of Divide country. The cows' movements are dominated by the presence of their offspring, which are born from mid-May to mid-June.

If winter ranges do not provide enough good feed, many of the calves may be aborted or be weak when born. Ratios of about 50 calves per 100 cows indicate good winter-range conditions. Low cow-calf ratios traditionally occur among the Continental Divide herds of the South Fork of the Flathead and the Sun River. These ranges have been over-browsed and often lack enough nourishment to support cows carrying calves through the rigors of winter. A challenge in elk management is to achieve the yearly hunting harvests needed to balance elk numbers to the winter ranges.

Cow-calf ratios tend to be higher east of the Divide, where winter conditions are more favorable. For example,

east of the Rocky Mountain Front the climax grasslands provide ample winter range. In the Flathead drainage west of the Divide, transitory winter ranges of brush fields are constantly being encroached upon by conifers. Here summer range is more plentiful than on the drier east side, but it is winter range that often limits game populations. The animals' learned migration patterns — those of both elk and deer — from east to west of the Divide may be influenced by the vast, only partially occupied summer habitat on the west side.

During 1935-1936 Forest Ranger L.J. Howard and his assistant C.A. McNeal conducted a game survey along the rugged Divide in the north end of the Bob Marshall Wilderness. Some of their wildlife observations are noteworthy:

44

"June 5. 4 elk and 3 grizzly bear seen on Elk Calf Mtn. on Two Medicine — Summit L.O. Trail ...

"June 10. 3 elk at east end of Big River Meadows, Flathead Forest. 1 elk on Continental Divide at head of S.F. Birch Creek. Indications show that some elk wintered at Gateway Gorge, and along the high divide between Big River Meadows and the heads of the Middle and South Forks of Birch Creek ...

"Wild Mountain Goats have been known to mix with a band of permitted domestic sheep on the North Badger Range on areas along the Continental Divide for a few days during mid-summer ...

"Mule deer would hang around areas [along the N.F. Sun River] where elk were pawing; after the elk had uncovered more or less feed, eaten some, wasted some, and left the area, the deer would utilize what was left or make use of the excavation pawed by the elk to uncover more feed, which would make it appear that the deer family are not so dumb."

The range of the 3,000-member Sun River elk herd encompasses some 1,200 square miles of rugged terrain in the upper reaches of the Sun River and on the western side of the Divide in the upper South and Middle Forks of the Flathead River. The east face of much of the Divide consists of 1,000' cliffs that confine the east-west migration to certain routes determined by passes through the limestone reefs. The 15-mile-long Chinese Wall is a barrier that can be crossed only through one minor pass. Elk can cross over four major and two minor passes through a series of cliffs north of the Chinese Wall. In the fall, they move across well-used migration trails from the head of the Middle Fork Flathead River and over Sun River Pass to the east side. By late June the elk are again moving back up the Sun River drainage when the calves are strong enough to make the trip.

There is another rough elk crossing at the head of the North Fork of Lick Creek into Hart Basin on the west side. Bob Cooney and a party of three once took horses over this steep notch in the Divide. There were fresh grizzly droppings in the trail on top of the Divide at this point. Possibly the great bear was lying in wait for an elk dinner to cross.

Wildlife biologist Harold Picton evaluated the hypothesis that early-season fall hunting west of the Divide causes the elk to migrate into the Sun River Game Preserve on the east side. After checking the major passes for tracks in 1957-1958, he concluded that the early season did not have any appreciable effect on elk migration.

Grizzly Bears

Symbolic of freedom and wildness along Montana's Continental Divide is the free-roaming grizzly bear. The awesome size and sometimes aggressive nature of this magnificent animal command a healthy respect.

With the European invasion of North America the range of the grizzly has continually receded. From the time of the Lewis and Clark Expedition, during which at least 43 of the great "white bears" were killed, bears have long been killed out of fear, for hides, and to protect livestock.

Now, with perhaps fewer than 1,000 grizzlies surviving south of Canada, the great bear is making his last stand along the most remote reaches of the northern Continental Divide ecosystem (Glacier Park and the Bob Marshall area) and the greater Yellowstone ecosystem. Those few remaining places that man has not converted to human uses — the wilderness stretches along Montana's Continental Divide — have become the last stronghold of the grizzly in the lower 48, where it is listed as a threatened species. This means that the bear and its habitat are supposed to be protected under the 1973 Endangered Species Act. The ultimate objective must be for the bear to recover to a viable, self-sustaining population so as to remove it from the list of threatened and endangered species.

Like us, grizzlies are omnivorous, so much so that John Muir once said that to the grizzly "almost everything is food except granite." Noted grizzly authority Dr. John Craighead observes that the bear needs three climatic zones: alpine, subalpine and temperate. The four major plant energy sources in the alpine and subalpine zones are grasses, forbs, berries and pine nuts. Grasses are chiefly spring and summer foods, berries almost exclusively summer foods and pine nuts mostly fall food in a normal year. The sure supply of grasses is a "survival ration" that carries the bear through times when the other foods are not available.

Along and near Montana's Divide country grizzlies hibernate from October/November until March/April. Adult grizzlies leave their winter dens in the spring, eating lightly for several weeks. As foods become more available, the bears' appetite and food consumption go up correspondingly. The deliberate routine of the bear's activities is linked to the emergence and maturation of plants.

In early June, elk begin dropping their calves in the temperate and subalpine parklands of Montana grizzly country. Grizzlies, whose home ranges encompass these traditional calving grounds, often locate elk by scent and

The grizzly bear frequents Divide country through the Glacier Park-Bob Marshall area and where the Divide abuts Yellowstone Park. MICHAEL FRANCIS

follow them as they migrate to these areas. The newborn calves are vulnerable to grizzlies for only a short time, after which the cows and their offspring move to higher elevations, depending on the recession of snow and the development of plants. The bears follow the same basic pattern, so that by July they are feeding on the grasses, sedges and forbs in both the subalpine and alpine zones. During July, grizzlies seem to crave insects such as moths, beetles, ants and even earthworms, although they may choose what is most available at the time. By August huckleberries are ripening in the temperate zone, and grizzlies gorge themselves on this food almost exclusively in a good berry year. In the fall, the nuts of the whitebark and limber pines become a critical energy source.

On several occasions I have seen extensive grizzly diggings along the west slope of the Chinese Wall, where the bears were looking for cow parsnips and glacier lilies.

Wolves. ALAN CAREY

Mountain lion—seldom seen, rarely heard. CRAIG SHARPE

This rooting and digging by the bears actually aids in plant growth by spreading seeds and aerating the soil.

During his grizzly bear habitat study in the Scapegoat Wilderness, John Craighead learned that the most important alpine habitat units along the Divide were the alpine meadow, alpine meadow krummholz, glacial cirque basin and mountain massif, all of which had an abundance of bear food plants exceeding 50 percent of the total ground cover.

There are numerous specific plants that are used by the bears at different times along the Divide. These include spring beauties, elk thistle, parsnip and succulent sedges and grasses. Most tuber plants, such as snakeroot, are preferred. Grizzlies consume an amazing variety of plants. Of these, two along the Divide are so heavily used that their relative absence in some years has a profound impact on bear behavior and distribution. These are whitebark pine nuts (in the fall) and huckleberries (mid-July to early September). Of course, nature is constantly varying the relative abundance of foods.

Until recently, the grizzly has survived because its spacious habitat needs have been protected by the remoteness and rugged topography of that habitat. These factors alone are no longer enough. Now, some of the last unprotected Continental Divide grizzly habitats, on the northern and southern ends of the Bob Marshall country and just west of Yellowstone Park, are under siege. If we are to secure the future of the great bear as part of our American wilderness legacy, we must stop chipping away at the last 2 percent of its native habitat, with "one more" timber road, gas well, or ski area.

John Craighead suggests that man has a moral obligation as well as a deep-seated psychological need to preserve a once co-dominant species. He points out that "the grizzly is one of the few inhabitants of our primeval environment that can, on occasion, remind us with lethal action that we are not and should not be immune masters of the wild places."

Dr. Craighead observes that with the low natural reproduction rate of the grizzly and the unacceptably high human-caused mortalities, protection of habitat is vital. He states flatly that "wilderness protection of the Northern Continental Divide ecosystem is essential" to the grizzly, and that "we would be a lot better off if every bit of the Rocky Mountain Front east of the Divide was put into the Bob Marshall Wilderness."

Mountain Lions

I've spent much of my life roaming the wildlands of the Northern Rockies and have caught only a fleeting glimpse of one of these highly secretive predators in all this time. Their nocturnal habits and shy nature mean that the cougar is seldom seen by people. Of course, this elusive nature is to be expected of an animal that survives by stalking and killing prey. It hunts deer and sometimes elk, but any hapless creature that crosses in front of a hungry cougar is apt to end up as its next meal.

Research in Idaho indicates that the home range of a mountain lion averages about 20 to 30 square miles, but may extend up to 100 square miles. Male lions have been known to kill and eat their unprotected offspring, although this is rare because females will defend their kittens with tooth and claw.

Once while camping under the Divide in the Bob Marshall Wilderness I was awakened by the hair-raising scream of a cougar in the night. I don't recall getting much sleep after that.

Wolves

Since 1983 at least 15 wolf sightings have been reported in the Badger/Two Medicine country near the Continental Divide just south of Glacier Park. The number of wolf reports places the Rocky Mountain Front second only to the North Fork of the Flathead as an area where wolf populations may recover. With abundant game for wolf food, the Divide country near and along the Front is a natural corridor for the movement of wolves to the south.

Wolves are quite social, traveling in packs with only the dominant male and female in a pack breeding. This wide-ranging animal may trot or run for long periods covering up to 45 miles a day. A pack may need a territory of 75 to 150 square miles, but it may be smaller in winter when the prey species are concentrated on winter ranges. The key is to have large remote expanses of country relatively free from humans and their uses.

Wolves depend on large ungulate populations. They have been known to follow elk to their high summer pastures and return with them to their winter range.

Wildland corridors, such as the northern Continental Divide, are important to the recovery of this endangered species. Someday a wolf recovery plan may protect wolves in remote wilderness areas, such as the Bob Marshall, but permit them to be shot if they cause trouble on private land. At present, it is illegal to kill wolves anywhere in Montana, even if they are killing livestock.

There is an interesting parallel between wolves and the 19th century plains Indians. Starting in the 1870s, it took only 15 years for the market hunters to wipe out the herds of buffalo — mainstay of both the Plains Indian and the wolf. As Montana wolf researcher Ursula Mattson put it, "wolves and Indians were caught under the wheels of Manifest Destiny. The Indians were squeezed onto reservations and the wolves were choked to oblivion in the West."

With an estimated five to seven wolves now living in the North Fork of the Flathead, the exciting potential for wolf recovery faces the uncertain future of increasing human intrusions into remote habitat near the Divide. I have never seen, or even heard, a wolf in the wild. But I hope that, some dark night beneath Montana's Great Divide, I might again be awakened by a primeval sound — not that of a screaming cougar but, rather, the chorus of a wild wolf pack.

Above: *Lynx kittens, about six weeks old.* ALAN CAREY
Left: *Yellow-bellied marmots basking in high mountain sun.*
MICHAEL FRANCIS

Year-Round Residents of the Divide

There are perhaps three major kinds of animal/bird groups found along the Continental Divide:
1. The seasonal "passers-by" species that happen to wander along or across the Divide just because it is there;
2. The migratory species who must deal with the Divide because of what it does to their enviroment. Here the Divide is a barrier to cross as well as a survival necessity.

After weather systems leave the deep-snow country on the west side, the Divide wrings out their moisture, making possible the open grasslands to the east; and
3. The high country alpine species that usually have small home ranges and may hibernate. Examples are the tiny rosy finches and the hibernating hoary marmots. We'll take a look at this latter group.

The mountain goat may be the most visible of such hardy souls, but don't underestimate that short-eared relative of the rabbit — the tiny pika. Instead of hibernating, this industrious little creature frantically gathers grasses in late summer. After the grass cures in the sun it is stored in the rocky crevice home of the pika along the crest of the Divide. The next time you hear the high-pitched "ka-ack, ka-ack" of the pika in a boulder field atop the Divide, think of the 30 pounds of dried grass that got that little five-ounce rabbit through the winter.

Marmots look something like a giant pika. They also live all year among the rock slides and peaks of the Divide. During the winter they burrow out a comfortable den and hibernate.

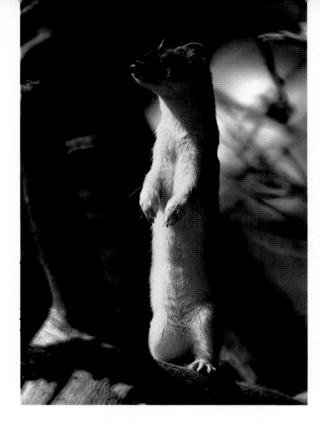

Birds of the Divide

More than any other bird, the delicate little rosy finch epitomizes the Great Divide. So many times I've seen this beautiful alpine aviator jumping from rock to rock amidst the harsh wind and spitting snow of a typical fall day along the Divide.

The great gray owl lives along the Divide, especially in lodgepole pine forests. Also some great horned owls favor alpine Divide habitat and pigmy owls move along and near the Divide from ponderosa pine forests up to the subalpine zone. Short-eared owls nest on the ground near the Divide.

Many raptors move south along the Divide from Canada and Alaska. They proceed when atmospheric conditions cause bright, sunny days with thermal updrafts that aid in soaring and flying. The birds are more easily observed during fall migration. These birds of prey may interrupt or even stop their migration if prey numbers are high enough. So, in a general sort of way, the Divide helps channel raptor migrations. Majestic golden eagles soar above the peaks and canyons throughout the year.

The varied birdlife along the Divide also includes the harlequin duck and goshawk, both of which I've observed near the high crest.

This discussion would not be complete without a glimpse of the endurance champion in the bird world — the white-tailed ptarmigan. This hardy little one-pound bird has adapted in several ways to survive year-round along and near Montana's harsh Divide country. The most familiar is the color change it undergoes each year. The mottled brown color of summer turns pure white by winter, a perfect blend for its snowbound alpine surroundings. Another adaptation is its feathered feet that act like snowshoes by providing more surface area for the bird to walk on in the snow. It spends the winter days feeding on dwarf willow. At night, the ptarmigan burrows into a snow cave that insulates it from the intense cold of the high Divide.

The presence of these marvelously adapted native birds and animals along and near the high crest is the best indicator that much of the country straddling the Continental Divide in Montana remains wild and free. With wise stewardship of our natural resources it will always remain so.

Top: *A long-tailed weasel, habitant of Divide forests.* MICHAEL QUINTON
Bottom: *Immature grouse on the Continental Divide just north of Lewis and Clark Pass.* BILL CUNNINGHAM

Top: *Ptarmigan showing spots of summer plumage through its white winter feathers.* BRUCE SELYEM
Center: *Golden eagle feeding young.* GUS WOLFE
Bottom: *Water ouzel, commonly known as a dipper, thrives in fast waterways along Montana's Divide.* MICHAEL QUINTON

Early Notes About Wildlife on the Divide

The period from 1810 to 1840 was the golden age of the Rocky Mountain fur trade. Adventurous bands of trappers wandered the entire region. There is not a stream on Montana's Continental Divide along whose length they did not set their traps. With the nearly complete extermination of the beaver in the 1840s, the fur trade began to ebb, leaving little trace on the country but having generated a knowledge of Montana's geography that facilitated subsequent settlement.

Captain Raynolds' military expedition of 1859-1860 gives us a picture of what much of the country was like before it was modified by the white man. His route completely encircled the site of present-day Yellowstone National Park, which was not officially explored until the Washburn-Doane expedition of 1870. Raynolds traveled up Henry's River to Henry's Lake, over the Divide, and into the Madison Basin. Here he found large numbers of elk, deer and antelope, as well as a band of buffalo in the high Madison Basin adjacent to the Divide.

The Stevens Expedition of 1853 to 1855 was exploring a route for a Pacific railroad from St. Paul to Puget Sound. Captain John Mullan set up a winter base at Cantonment in the Bitterroot Valley, and by the end of 1855 every valley and mountain pass along the Divide within the region had been traced out and mapped. In December 1853 Mullan found plenty of buffalo in the Big Hole Basin just east of the Divide, as had Alexander Ross in March 1824. Most likely, the huge ungulates wintered in this 6,000'-high valley. Since the arrival of the white man there have been no native buffalo west of the Continental Divide, though they formerly lived there. In Governor Stevens' 1853 report, Dr. Suckley writes, "Buffalo were formally [*sic*] in great numbers in this valley [Bitterroot] as attested by the number of skulls seen, and by the reports of the inhabitants. For a number of years past, none had been seen west of the mountains, but singular to relate, a buffalo bull was killed at the mouth of the Pend Oreille River on the day I passed it. The Indians were in great joy over this, believing that the buffalo were coming back to them."

In 1824 the Ross party of free trappers encountered elk, deer and mountain goats in the mountains near the Divide

above the Bitterroot Valley. The group was delayed by deep snow in Ross Hole. For about a month they subsisted mainly on mountain sheep, which were abundant in the mountains along the Divide.

A notion has long endured that before the coming of the white man the mountains were thinly populated with game, and that it was only through heavy hunting on the plains that the animals were driven into the mountains for refuge. This theory is based largely on Lewis and Clark's record of the lack of game in the mountains and on a half dozen reports of early exploration in Yellowstone from 1870 to 1875.

I do not accept this theory. It is likely based on relative rather than actual numbers of wildlife in the mountains as compared to the plains. It is probably true that elk and buffalo were primarily plains animals in that they occurred in far greater numbers in the prairie country. Likewise, mountain sheep were much more abundant in the Missouri Breaks than they ever were in the high timberline country near the Divide. But there is good evidence that these animals also ranged the high mountainous Divide country in greater numbers than they have at any time since the valleys were settled. In other words, the plains animals were killed off, not driven back into the mountains. Meanwhile, the rougher mountain country continued to give some refuge to the animals that were already there.

Bob Cooney— Pioneer Wildlife Biologist

Bob Cooney first went into the Bob Marshall country along the Divide in 1934 on a winter-range survey in the Sun River for the Forest Service. His firsthand knowledge of the wilderness and wildlife of Montana's Continental Divide extends back more than half a century. Here Bob expresses his feelings for the central spine of the wilderness:

"The Continental Divide in Montana has always held a special meaning for me. This great mountain crest separating the Pacific from the Atlantic drainages within the Bob Marshall Wilderness Country has been my favorate part of it. Many memories come back — fresh diggings for

fleshy roots by grizzly bears on high Divide slopes near timberline have been reminders that this country is truly wild and remote. Few trails contact the Divide — following its crest even on foot is no easy task. In addition to the evidence of grizzlies and mountain goats we were always interested in well-worn elk migration trails that crossed the Divide here and there at strategic places. We followed these trails many times in efforts to learn as much as possible about the elk that summered well back in the high Divide country."

Canada geese. ALAN CAREY

Of Geese and Winter

Late one hunting season, with heavy snows already beginning to pile up in the basins below the Divide, noted Montana conservationist Jim Posewitz was hunting elk in the austere, mostly treeless Lima Peaks Divide country of southwest Montana. Jim had sweated his way to a high pass along the crest. Suddenly, to the northeast and far below he spotted a wedge of Canada geese slowing ascending the steep basin slopes. The geese appeared suspended in time and space as they battled against severe wind, altitude, cold and driving snow. Only the incessant wind could be heard as the determined waterfowl beat their great wings, flying toward the headwaters of the Pacific. Perhaps they had just left nesting islands in the Missouri River, or maybe they had traveled from the Arctic. The complete silence of the great birds seemed to underscore their determination. At last, a mere 20 yards from Jim, the flock topped the Divide and exploded in joyous sound. It was as though they were celebrating their passage from winter across the last great barrier to the comparatively mild climate of the Snake River plains far below.

PART II

People Along the Divide

Shaping the Character of the State

Human traverse and use of the Continental Divide in Montana began long before recorded history, but little evidence remains from its use prior to the Lewis and Clark Expedition of 1804-1806. We do know that native peoples made use of portions of the Divide for centuries before the advent of European man. This mostly seasonal use was largely a function of favorable weather conditions because the Divide was, as it is now, a harsh environment not conducive to settlement or even extended camping.

This look into the past will focus on some of the isolated happenings, stories, and locales along the Divide that have added so much drama and life to Montana's colorful history. Indeed, the history of the Divide is a microcosm of the history of Montana. Mining camps (and their generally rapid evolution to ghost towns) sprang up close to the Continental Divide because of the mineralization of high mountain streams and rock outcroppings. The Divide was that continuous, omnipresent physical obstacle that had to be overcome by those who would explore, trap, mine, log, build railroads and highways, or just plain get from east to west and vice versa. As such, some of Montana's richest history flows from the high crest as surely as the runoff from the melting snowbank in spring. We will sample some of this richness as we look at Indians, explorers, boundary surveys, mining camps, railroads, early roads and highways and even a bit of humor.

Blackfeet Indians in today's Glacier National Park ride a mountain trail used by their ancestors. MONTANA HISTORICAL SOCIETY

Opposite page: *Surrounded by cottonwoods and conifers at Rogers Pass, one wonders what stories this old trapper's cabin could tell.* GEORGE WUERTHNER

E.S. Shipp photographed this stockade in 1920; it had been used by early white settlers in the Big Hole Basin of southwestern Montana.
U.S. FOREST SERVICE

The Rich History of Lemhi Pass

When the Lemhi Shoshones obtained horses in the 18th century, Lemhi Pass became more important as the route connecting the two major parts of their homeland, Lemhi Valley and the Big Hole Basin, along with nearby portions of the upper Missouri River Valley. They used the pass in their annual migration from salmon fishing west of the Divide to buffalo hunting on the east side. These hunting trips were made in the fall to prevent the spoilage of meat and hides. Before they acquired horses, the Indians made use of buffalo jumps and walled traps, some of which have been found at the head of the Beaverhead Valley.

After the mounted Blackfeet began to range farther south and west, they regularly used Lemhi Pass to access the upper Snake River Valley. By 1824 Alexander Ross referred to the Lemhi Pass route as the "Blackfoot Road."

The fur trappers (1810-1845) also used Lemhi Pass to reach the Snake River country. In 1823 Finan MacDonald fought a major battle with the Blackfeet close to the pass. In 1829 an expedition led by Jedediah Smith crossed Lemhi Pass while en route from the Pacific Northwest to St. Louis.

In 1855 the Mormon Church founded a colony on the Lemhi River. "Limhi" is a character from the Book of Mormon, known as King Limhi. Later settlers misspelled the word to develop "Lemhi."

For a while, the pass was used to transport freight into Lemhi County, Idaho. However, the building of the Gilmore and Pittsburgh Railroad from Armstead, Montana, to Salmon, Idaho, via nearby Bannack Pass brought the traffic over Lemhi Pass almost to a standstill. During the summer of 1985 the Beaverhead National Forest began construction of a higher-standard gravel road up to the Divide. Still, this historic grassy pass remains much as Lewis and Clark first saw it nearly two centuries ago.

Indians and the European Invasion of Their Homeland

Those who first traveled along Montana's Continental Divide remain a mystery. The prehistoric hunters of thousands of years ago have left little evidence of their activity. A few tipi rings, ancient campsites, and tool artifacts are scattered atop and near portions of the Divide, mostly near and south of Lewis and Clark Pass. Several of the 27 known prehistoric sites in Glacier National Park are close to the Divide, some of which date back to about 1000 B.C. Certain mountain passes in Glacier were used as travel corridors for Blackfeet raiding parties, and for Kutenai, Kalispel, and Flathead tribal migrations to the Great Plains for seasonal buffalo hunts. Unlike most of Montana, many place names in the park are of Indian derivation, although they were assigned to park features by the Great Northern Railway for promotional purposes.

The powerful Blackfeet dominated the entire upper Missouri region during the late 1700s after they had obtained horses and guns. For them, the northern Continental Divide served as a massive western boundary. But they utilized the high passes to send small raiding parties across the Divide to prey upon tribes of the western slope. Rarely did the Blackfeet hunt in the mountains since their lifestyle was geared to the prairie.

The early Plains Indians viewed the crest of the mountains as the limits of the earth, where the most powerful rivers have their sources. They called the high crest the "bridge of the world" where the Great Spirit resides. Some of the tribes saw the mountains as their dwelling place after death, where they would climb the steepest peaks. After months of fatigue and danger they would reach the land of shades at the summit. They would then see the souls of good Indians living in beautiful tents, pitched in a field of luxuriant verdure, watered by shining rivulets, and filled with buffalo, elk and deer.

Less militaristic tribes, such as the Kutenai, Kalispel, and Flathead were more accustomed to the mountains, having been forced there by the Blackfeet. Once or twice a year, hunting parties from these western mountain tribes ventured east across the Divide to hunt buffalo at the risk of Blackfeet attack. Marias was one of the major early passes through which the western tribes crossed the mountains. Ambushes by the Blackfeet caused the western Indians to swing farther north to Cut Bank, Red Eagle, and other more difficult but safer travel corridors.

Even these passes were not entirely safe, as evidenced by a clash around 1810 to 1812 near Cut Bank Pass. As some Kutenai were returning westward, Mad Wolf and his band of Blackfeet killed and scalped all of the Kutenai except for one old woman. Despite such occasional hazards, the western tribes were amazingly well-adapted to the mountains. The Kutenai could actually run down mountain sheep on foot. Early white settlers noted the large size of their leg muscles from climbing the steep ridges.

The first recorded use of Marias Pass by white men was in 1810 when Northwester David Thompson reported in his journals that a band of 150 Flathead Indians, accompanied by three white traders, traversed the mountains by a "wide defile of easy passage eastward of Salish [Flathead] Lake, to hunt buffalo and make dried provisions." Just west of the Divide the party was attacked by 170 Piegans and a furious battle followed. The Flatheads had been tipped off and had time to fortify their positions. In addition, David Thompson had armed them with 20 guns and several hundred iron arrow points. Three horseback charges were easily turned back. The infuriated attackers tried to lure the Flatheads into the open by darting about on foot thereby making themselves hard to hit with the old-style muskets. Sixteen Piegans reportedly died.

Their defeat at Marias Pass added to the Blackfeet Nation's anger against white men, which had been fueled by their meeting with Lewis and Clark Expedition members only a few years previously. The Blackfeet served notice that any white people found east of the mountains would be treated as enemies. The Flatheads aggravated the situation by bragging widely about their victory at Marias.

David Thompson also mentions a battle that took place about 1811 near the mouth of Morrison Creek, a short distance west of the Divide in what is today the Great Bear Wilderness. The Blackfeet reportedly inflicted heavy losses on the Flathead.

After an unsuccessful peace attempt, the Flatheads in 1812 sent a hunting party east over Cut Bank Pass. They were accompanied by two French free trappers, Michael Bourdeaux and Michael Kinville. The Piegans were guarding the eastern approaches to the pass and a running battle broke out. Both white men and many Indians on both sides were killed. Somewhere on Cut Bank Creek there was reported to be a great pile of rocks covering the bones of Flathead Indians who died long ago at the hands of the Piegans. This may well have been the site of the 1812 battle.

After this fight, the Piegans became even more warlike as they relentlessly tried to wipe out any small native parties that they could find. They placed sentries at high points to guard the eastern approaches to the passes, especially Marias. With Marias Pass effectively closed, the better protected passes to the north and south were used even more. The hostility of the Blackfeet Nation and the natural fear of western Indian guides explain why later expeditions were unable to locate the easiest route across the mountains for the next 75 years. Over time the trail across Marias was blocked by grass and downed timber. Only the more adventuresome or foolhardy traversed the pass, and few of them left any record.

Unlike Forest Service trails through the mountains, Indian travel corridors conformed to natural routes that took advantage of open ridges and game trails. There were several major Indian trails across the Divide south of Marias Pass in the Bob Marshall Wilderness. One of the routes crossed the Divide at the head of the Middle Fork of the Flathead River and headed northeast to Marias Pass. Another trail went up the Middle Fork of the Flathead to the head of Lodgepole Creek, and then over the Divide into the

This placid site along the North Fork of the Big Hole River witnessed the furious August 9, 1877, Battle of the Big Hole. JEFF GNASS

Right top: *Badger Pass was on one of the favored Indian routes across the mountains to the buffalo on the plains.* SYLVIA JOSLIN
Right bottom: *Big River Meadows and Gateway Pass define one of the important historic Indian routes across the Divide. It became popular when the Blackfeet closed the lower Marias Pass route to western tribes around 1812.* RICK GRAETZ
Below: *Here, near the mouth of Cabin Creek about 1840, Flathead Indians ambushed a band of surprised Blackfeet— only a few miles west of the Continental Divide.* BILL CUNNINGHAM

Two Medicine drainage. A third major Indian trail crossed through Big River Meadows, over Gateway Pass and down into the South Fork of Birch Creek. To the south, an important Indian route left the Danaher River, crossed over Camp Creek Pass through Pearl Basin and proceeded to the Sun River on its way to the prairie.

This last trail was the site of a major battle between two tribes about 1840. The Flatheads had been east of the mountains and were returning with their buffalo meat and a few extra horses. They were camped near Basin Creek above Big Prairie in the present-day Bob Marshall Wilderness. One of their scouts stormed into the camp and announced that a large number of Blackfeet were

approaching the Divide from the east. The women and children hastily moved the camp downstream to Big Prairie. The Flathead warriors positioned themselves near the mouth of Camp Creek and sprung a successful ambush that almost wiped out the surprised Blackfeet.

The Flatheads called the Blackfoot River "Cokalahishkit" —river of the road to the buffalo. Use of this historic trail, a continuation of the Lolo Trail near Missoula, dates far back into prehistory. Alice Creek, just south of the Scapegoat Wilderness, was a major Indian camping site on this important road. Today, the remains of the trail consist of highly visible parallel grooves along Alice Creek and over the Divide at Lewis and Clark Pass, created from centuries

of use by the travois that the Indians pulled behind their horses. This is the route by which Indian guides took Meriwether Lewis and his men across the Divide on his return trip from the Pacific on July 7, 1806.

Perhaps the most famous battle between Indians and whites near the Continental Divide was the Battle of the Big Hole on August 9, 1877. During the summer of 1877 Chief Joseph and his band of about 800 Nez Perces fled from the U.S. Army, over a four-month period, from the tip of eastern Oregon to the Bear Paw Mountains just south of Canada. The Army was under orders to place the Indians on a reservation in western Idaho Territory. Hoping to escape peaceably, the Nez Perces were forced into a major battle with Colonel John Gibbon's advance party in the Big Hole Valley just east of Gibbons Pass.

Shortly before dawn on August 9 the soldiers and civilian volunteers crossed the west bank of the Big Hole River and began a surprise attack. The soldiers soon occupied the camp, but the Indian warriors found sniping positions and began picking off Gibbon's men with deadly accuracy. The soldiers were pinned down for two days while Chief Joseph hurriedly led his people southward. The Nez Perces paid a high price for their military victory over Gibbon, with 40 women, children and old people killed in the early morning attack, and 30 warriors lost in the fighting. Even more shattering was the realization that the Army was not going to let them go in peace.

With the nearly complete elimination of the buffalo and the rapid expansion of white settlement in Montana the stage was set for the demise of the free-roaming Indian. The Reservation Era was beginning and with this development several other events are noteworthy.

In 1885 George Bird Grinnell, noted naturalist and editor of the outdoor magazine *Forest and Stream,* made his first visit to what was to become Glacier National Park. He developed not only a deep love for the park area, but also a close friendship with the Blackfeet as well.

In the 1890s the federal government began negotiating with the Blackfeet for purchase of today's Glacier Park east of the Continental Divide. Grinnell served as a negotiator. The tribe eventually agreed to surrender title for $1.5 million worth of goods and services to be paid in annual installments over 10 years. Following purchase of this area, known as the Ceded Strip, the country was added to the immense Lewis and Clark Forest Reserve. The subsequent establishment of Glacier Park as we know it today would have been impossible without this spectacular mountain region east of the Divide.

Lewis and Clark Pass (6,323'), looking east, was used by Indians for centuries before Captain Lewis and his men crossed it on July 7, 1806.

View from Lewis and Clark Pass to the west in the Alice Creek basin. U.S. FOREST SERVICE PHOTOS

Early Pathfinders Across the Great Divide

The early exploration of the northern Continental Divide country is really the story of events in other places to which the Divide was a great barrier. The mountain crest was a formidable obstacle, generally regarded as a dangerous and hungry interlude for travelers. It was to be avoided or endured. Most thinkers of the time held tight to the dream of the Northwest Passage and easy navigation from east coast to west. After all, who could have imagined an unbroken chain that extended from Spanish observations in the south, beyond those of the British in the north all the way into Alaska?

Lewis and Clark

Meriwether Lewis for a decade had longed to have a chance to solve the Missouri-Columbia mystery. When President Jefferson discussed a plan to explore westward, Lewis lit up like the sun and the Lewis and Clark Expedition was born. In January 1803 the expedition was secretly approved by Congress. Three months later, in a deal so stunning as still to be almost beyond belief, Jefferson more than doubled United States territory by purchasing virtually the entire Great Plains region from France for $15 million. Jefferson instructed Lewis " ... to explore the Missouri river, and such principal stream of it, as by it's course and communication with the waters of the Pacific Ocean, may offer the most direct and practicable water communication across the continent, for the purposes of commerce."

There had long been speculation that there was a "Northwest Passage," a gap in the "cordillera" through which a water route led to the Pacific. Montana was in the unknown zone between New Mexico and the Canadian explorations of Alexander Mackenzie and Peter Fidler, who got as far south as the 50th Parallel just north of Montana. St. Louis traders firmly believed that the Missouri could be ascended as a navigable stream to within 100 miles of the Pacific.

On June 8, 1805, the expedition reached the mouth of the Marias River (named by Lewis for the woman he hoped to marry, Maria Wood). It was here that they became the first white men to record seeing the Montana Rockies — the 8,000-foot high barrier of the Lewis Range rose in blue majesty some 110 miles to the west. Lewis ascended about 30 miles up the Marias to the north while Clark scouted the southern fork.

In what was one of the most important decisions of the exploration, both men concluded that the south-trending Missouri was the main branch. In so deciding, they abandoned the hope of a short passage from the navigable Missouri to the navigable Columbia beyond the Continental Divide. The immense mass to the west was too high and wide for that. Ironically, had they proceeded incorrectly up the Marias, they might have found a far easier and shorter crossing of the mountains by way of Marias Pass.

As the expedition headed up the Missouri, the captains longed for horses. With them they could have searched for possible passes directly west, up the Sun or Dearborn

Rivers (today's Lewis and Clark, Cadotte and Rogers Passes).

On July 25 the head of the Missouri River at Three Forks was reached, 2,465 miles from St. Louis. The forks were named the Jefferson, Madison and Gallatin. It was carefully decided to follow the most westerly branch — the Jefferson. With game growing scarce and the ominous mountain mass looming to the west it was now a matter of urgency to find Indians who might guide them to the best passage.

Sacajawea, the young Shoshone Indian woman on the expedition, had been kidnapped from a village west of the Divide and said she was certain that she could find the way from the Missouri headwaters to her home. On August 3 the expedition went by Pipestone Creek just east of Pipestone Pass. From there they entered the vast grasslands of the Big Hole. As they passed the mouth of the Big Hole River, Lewis named it Wisdom in honor of one of Jefferson's traits.

On August 8, while on the Beaverhead River, Lewis saw indications of a pass (Lemhi) over the Bitterroots 60 miles to the northwest. At daybreak the excited Captain hurried ahead on foot with three of his men, resolving not to return until the Shoshone Indians were found. Securing horses from the Indians had become an absolute necessity. Toward the head of the Beaverhead River they had an agonizing glimpse of a single Indian, but the frightened native fled on horseback toward Lemhi Pass. They had not seen another human for four months.

On August 12 Lewis followed a winding Indian trail into the Bitterroot Range "which took us to the most distant fountain of the waters of the mighty Missouri," he wrote in his journal. One of the men joyfully stood astride the narrow stream just east of the pass and thanked God he had lived to bestride the Missouri. A short distance beyond, they reached 7,373' Lemhi Pass, and crossed the Continental Divide. They stopped at a small stream on the Pacific slope (in Idaho) to taste water of the great Columbia River. Lewis proclaimed, "I had accomplished one of those great objectives on which my mind had been unalterably fixed for many years."

On August 13 they at last met the Shoshones on the western slope during a "tense, disaster-charged time." The startled Indians became convinced of the friendly intentions of the explorers and returned across Lemhi Pass with Lewis to meet the main party with horses. The suspense ended on August 17 when it was learned that they had met the very band from which Sacajawea had been stolen, and that their chief, Cameahwait, was her brother — an incredible coincidence! Victory at Lemhi on the Continental Divide very likely made the difference between success and failure for the Lewis and Clark Expedition to the Pacific Coast.

Fortunate Camp was established at the mouth of Horse Prairie Creek, where the two captains bartered for horses with the Shoshones. Clark then took a few men over Lemhi Pass to search for the best route westward. On August 26 Lewis led the main party over the Divide via Lemhi Pass. It was on this third crossing that one of the Indian women lagged behind. She caught up about an hour later and proudly displayed the baby to whom she had given birth on top of the Continental Divide.

Lewis rejoined Clark at the Shoshone village in the Lemhi Valley of Idaho on August 29. They learned from the Indians that their best hope for crossing the Bitterroots to the west was the Lolo Trail, which was used by the Nez Perce Indians to reach the buffalo plains east of the Divide.

It was at this point that the expedition left the United States as represented by the Louisiana Purchase and entered Spanish territory. Of the three Continental Divide passes crossed by the expedition (Lemhi, Gibbons and Lewis and Clark), Lemhi is the only one over which both Lewis and Clark traveled.

The next crossings of the Great Divide followed the July 3, 1806, separation of the two captains at Traveler's Rest on the Bitterroot River near the mouth of Lolo Creek — a parting that Lewis hoped would be "only momentary." Lewis rode northward toward the Blackfoot River with two Nez Perce guides who had agreed to go as far as "the river on the road to the buffalo." Clark took the trail up the Bitterroot that led to the Continental Divide. This was the only time that the party split, as they searched for a better pass across the great mountain barrier.

On July 6, 1806, Clark wrote that "We then went along the creek [Camp Creek] for three miles, and leaving to the right the path by which we came last fall, pursued the road taken by the Ootlashoots [a Flathead band], up a jintle ascent to the dividing mountain which separates the waters of the middle fork of Clark's river, from those of Wisdom and Lewis' river. On the other side, we came to Glade Creek [Trail Creek] down which we proceeded, crossing it frequently into the glades on each side, where the timber is small, and in many places destroyed by fire .... Along these roads there are also appearances of old buffalo paths .... the coincidence of a buffalo [road] with an Indian road was the strongest assurance that it was the best."

Clark had crossed the Divide on the level, heavily-forested ridge of Gibbons Pass, which cut off about 60 miles from the route the expedition had followed the previous fall. It is interesting to note that the Continental Divide had not been crossed the previous fall even though Lewis and Clark topped the crest of the Bitterroots only three miles to the southwest. One of the Divide's many quirks is its abrupt northeasterly departure from the Bitterroots between Chief Joseph Pass and Gibbons Pass.

Meanwhile, the Lewis party of ten was making good time on the shortcut trail to the east, up the Big Blackfoot River.

Eleven miles east of the current town of Lincoln, the boiling Blackfoot River forked — Alice Creek to the left and Cadotte Creek to the right. Lewis chose the Alice Creek trail, based on the earlier recommendation of his Nez Perce guides. The trail took the Lewis detachment 14 miles to the woody top of the Continental Divide — 6,323' Lewis and Clark Pass — on July 7, 1806. From here, Lewis could see the distinctive Haystack Butte and the Missouri River Valley. The next day, as the party dropped down to the plains, they abandon the well-worn trail to hunt. They were once again in the country of plentiful game.

The unhappiest and most dangerous portion of the entire expedition occurred near the end. On July 17, Lewis headed north, determined to follow the Marias River to its source. Lewis wanted to discover whether there were passes at this northern latitude more favorable than those by which they had crossed the Divide farther south. It was at this point that the Marias bent to the southwest, so the river clearly did not attain as high a latitude as Lewis had previously assumed. He got as far as a point on Cut Bank Creek, about 12 miles northeast of present-day Browning. It was here at Camp Disappointment that the group spent four frustrating rainy days waiting for the sky to clear so longitudinal readings could be taken. On July 26 Lewis encountered a group of eight members of the warlike Piegan tribe. During an ensuing skirmish two of the Indians were killed and Lewis himself narrowly escaped death. Lewis's party fled to the Missouri, fearing retaliation from a larger band of Blackfeet.

The Lewis and Clark Expedition truly ranks as one of history's most exciting adventures. During the course of its epic journey, the entourage crossed seven major Rocky Mountain passes, all of them in Montana. Of these, three are on the main dividing ridge of the Rockies: Lemhi, Gibbons, and Lewis and Clark.

Alexander Ross

Alexander Ross was an early fur hunter in the Rocky Mountains, after whom "Ross Hole" in the upper East Fork of the Bitterroot River is named. That is where Ross and a large fur brigade camped in March 1824. As Ross and his party entered the place that now bears his name he " ... gazed in wonder at the bold and stupendous front ... which in every direction seemed to bid defiance to our approach. This gloomy and discouraging spot we reached on the 12th of March, 1824, and named this place 'The Valley of Troubles'."

The next morning Ross led a party in search of a pass through the mountains. They followed a small stream

about four miles to its head, "the source of the Flathead River," but could not find a pass because of heavy timber and snow that was seven feet deep on top.

Several days later a hunting party with the Ross brigade returned to the "Valley of Troubles" after a six-day absence and reported on its journey across the Continental Divide: "From the head of the creek we proceeded across the mountain in a southeasterly direction. The first three miles were thickly wooded, and the snow from six to eight feet deep, with a strong crust on the top. Afterwards, the country became more open, with occasional small prairies here and there; the snow, however, keeping the same depth, with the crust still harder and harder on the top as we advanced, for about three miles further, till we had reached fully the middle of the mountain.

"From thence, all along to the other side, a distance of six miles more, the snow ranged from five to six feet deep, with the crust very strong, till we got to the open plains. The distance, therefore, across, is twelve long miles — a distance and depth of snow that can never be passed with horses in its present state. Beyond the mountain is a large open plain [Big Hole Basin] over which the snow is scarcely a foot deep. There we found plenty of buffalo, sixteen of which we killed; but for want of wood and other materials we could not make stages to preserve the meat, but had to abandon it to the wolves, excepting the little we have brought with us."

When Ross finally did make it over Gibbons Pass into the Big Hole Valley he eventually worked his way into Horse Prairie and over Lemhi Pass into the Lemhi Valley. From there he circled back through Bannack Pass into Horse Prairie on a trapping expedition that was " ... the most profitable ever to come out of the country in one year; amounting to 5000 beaver, exclusive of other peltries."

Charles Geyer

In 1843 botanist Charles Geyer, his collecting expedition sponsored by Scots nobleman Sir William Drummond Stewart, entered Montana near Targhee Pass and descended the Madison River. Later, he again crossed the Continental Divide moving from the Big Hole over Gibbons Pass to the Bitterroot Valley. Larry Thompson, in *Montana's Explorers: The Pioneer Naturalists*, quotes Geyer's description of the Beaverhead country as the "green desert, cold and inhospitable ... " But the "green mountains" of the Bitterroots left Geyer with a far different impression as did the "verdant" Bitterroot Valley. The

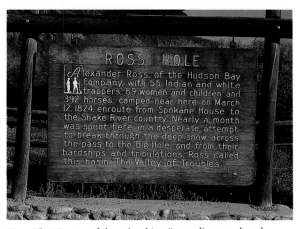

Top: *The "Queen of the columbines" was discovered and described by English botanist Joseph Burke near the Continental Divide in the Lima Peaks.* BRUCE SELYEM
Bottom: *Fur trapper Alexander Ross and his party spent a gloomy and hungry winter in the "Valley of Troubles" before conditions allowed them to cross over the Continental Divide to the Big Hole.* BILL CUNNINGHAM

botanist was one of the first to scientifically note forest succession, Thompson points out, as he observed pioneer forest species occupying the space after a fire. He also took note of the Bannock Indians who sometimes frequented the upper Beaverhead country near the Divide. The

Bannocks "live the most wretched life of any Indians in the West .... Oftentimes, when they can get neither game nor roots to live on, they eat grasshoppers ... very large and fat, of every shade of brown and black, wherewith these deserts abound."

Joseph Burke

Burke was an English botanist exploring North America under the sponsorship of the 13th Earl of Derby. As Thompson explains in *Montana's Explorers,* Burke entered Montana on July 5, 1845, over a nameless pass on the Divide near the Lima Peaks. While camping nearby Burke discovered a flower that left a lasting impression. "In that place I found a most beautiful Columbine. Flowers are very large and beautyfully white, with varieties shaded a clear light blue — In my opinion it is not only the Queen of Columbines, but the most beautiful of all herbaceous plants." Later that summer, upon returning to the Snake River country, Burke decided that he had to go back to the Lima Peaks and collect seeds from the "Queen of Columbines." He separated from the main party and ascended the pass, traveling alone in hostile Indian country to obtain precious seeds of the Colorado columbine.

How the Crest of the Bitterroots Became the Western Boundary of Montana

As a boy I was told the common story of how a surveyor's error accounted for the western boundary of Montana being located along the crest of the Bitterroot Mountains instead of along the Continental Divide farther east. Indeed, with the division between the crest of the Bitterroots and the Continental Divide just north of Chief Joseph Pass being almost indistinguishable on the ground, it is easy to see how such a mistake could have been made.

However, the real reason for Montana's having any land at all west of the Divide is because of the politicking of the man who would become the first territorial governor — Sidney Edgerton.

In 1863, Idaho Territory was created, covering all of present-day Idaho, Montana and Wyoming. President Abraham Lincoln appointed Ohio politician Sidney Edgerton as Chief Justice of the new territory and Edgerton set out for the territorial capital of Lewiston, I.T. He got as far as Bannack, where he learned that the territorial governor had assigned him to the Idaho Territory's easternmost judicial district — despite his status as Chief Justice.

Even so, the onset of winter weather would have kept Edgerton in Bannack that fall. Travel through the Deer Lodge Valley, over the Divide and then across the width of modern Idaho was impossible at least eight months each year. The miners and merchants pouring into Bannack and Virginia City believed their seat of government was too far away to be effective. Henry Plummer's road agents made the most of the situation.

Not surprisingly, Edgerton aligned himself with the movement to create a Montana Territory. Also not surprisingly, Grasshopper Creek and Alder Gulch residents were happy to send this former congressman to the nation's capital to plead their case — before a president and representatives he personally knew. His friend and fellow Ohioan, James Ashley, merely happened to be chairman of the House Committee on Territories.

Edgerton headed east in January 1864, only four months after he had first arrived in Bannack. He was certainly not a lone crusader for the cause: The Idaho territorial legislature already had petitioned Congress to divide the vast territory along the Continental Divide. Idaho's congressional delegate (and former territorial governor) William Henson Wallace joined Edgerton in testifying before the Committee on Territories, emphasizing the need for government located east of the Divide to serve the rapidly increasing population there.

But while the powerful Ashley was smoothing the passage of a bill creating Montana Territory, Edgerton went after more land. Montana's border was pushed westward from the Divide, to the crest of the Bitterroots. Montana Territory, as created, included three fourths of the Idaho panhandle. The Idaho territorial legislature would try in vain to have Congress return the boundary to the Continental Divide.

During his return to Montana in July 1864 Edgerton learned that President Lincoln had appointed him Governor of Montana Territory. The political fortune of Governor Wallace was not as bright. As a result of Wallace's having agreed to give up part of Idaho to Montana, the incensed voters defeated him for Congress in the next election.

Explorer-naturalists Joseph Burke and Father DeSmet likely traveled across subalpine fields like this meadow of wild iris along the East Fork of Little Sheep Creek below Mount Garfield, Lima Peaks. GEORGE WUERTHNER

Father Pierre Jean De Smet

This Jesuit priest was a tireless wilderness wanderer who traveled some 180,000 miles on foot and horseback, much of it in Montana. Father De Smet joined the American Fur Company's annual expedition in 1840 from St. Louis to the Rocky Mountains. He left the party in eastern Idaho and entered what is now Montana over the Continental Divide between Henry's Lake to Red Rock Lakes, probably through Red Rock Pass. He wrote extensively of Montana lands, vegetation and wild inhabitants — including those of the Continental Divide country. Father De Smet is perhaps best known for establishing St. Mary's Mission near Stevensville, the first permament white settlement in Montana.

De Smet called the Missouri "my river," because of his numerous travels up and down its course. " ... I have drunk the limpid waters of its sources, and the muddy waters at its mouth, distant more than three thousand miles from each other ..." (quoted in Thompson, *Montana Explorers*)

John Mullan

One of Isaac Stevens' most capable lieutenants, Mullan directed the U.S. Army's 624-mile-long overland wagon-road project, connecting Fort Benton with Fort Walla Walla. In 1860 this first officially surveyed road in the Northern Rockies was completed. The survey produced not only an important transmountain link, but also more comprehensive knowledge of the region.

Mullan gives the following description of his namesake pass over the Continental Divide: "You approach and descend this pass by a gradual slope; the summit is not

timbered, the mountains on both sides are much higher and densely timbered with fir and pine, it is 6000 feet above the level of the sea and is evidently one of the lowest depressions in the whole range. — On the morning of July 17th, we crossed the range at Mullan's Pass without difficulty and camped upon the waters of the Missouri."

The Mullan Road was used extensively by immigrants, miners, and travelers until completion of the Northern Pacific Railroad in 1883. In 1865 Captain Mullan published a *Miners and Travelers' Guide* in which he recommends a 47-day itinerary for traveling the 624 miles of his road, "or, allowing 18 days for delays, contingencies, and recruiting animals, in 55 days, with loaded wagons; or in 30 days if you are traveling with pack animals."

Mullan explicitly describes the crossing of the Continental Divide:

"THIRTY-SEVENTH DAY — Move to west base of Rocky Mountains, at Mullan's Pass, thirteen and a half miles; road generally good, though sometimes wet in early spring; no ascending the north fork of Little Blackfoot; wood, water, and grass at camp.
"THIRTY-EIGHTH DAY — Cross summit of Rocky Mountains and go seven miles to Fir Creek; road good; wood, water and grass at camp."

A century later a traveler writes, "We were exceptionally fortunate to ... be on Mullan Pass almost exactly one hundred years after Mullan and his party built the road over it. A short distance north is a monument commemorating the site of the first Masonic meeting held in Montana. A plaque attached to the native rock altar reads, 'On September 23rd, 1862, the first Masonic Meeting in Montana was held here,' we have been informed that meetings are held here every summer, sponsored by the different Masonic Lodges in this area. This is truly an inspiring spot, little changed over the past hundred years. The old [Mullan] road winds its way down Big Prickly Pear Creek to the railroad station of Austin."

Northwest Boundary Survey—49th Parallel Across the Divide

The Oregon Treaty of 1846 established the 49th Parallel as the "line of boundary between the territories of the United States and those of her Britannic Majesty." Prior to this agreement, Great Britain claimed land as far south as the northern border of California, and the United States claimed territory as far north as southern Alaska at the 54-degree 40-minute parallel. The U.S. slogan was "Fifty-four forty or fight," but there was no fight and no fifty-four forty.

A decade later Congress passed an act authorizing the official survey and marking of the international boundary from the Pacific Ocean to the Continental Divide. Archibald Campbell was appointed United States Commissioner. The Campbell party went directly to Oregon Territory and were in the field by the summer of 1857. The party's British counterpart, under Colonel J.S. Hawkins, began work the following spring. The British and American land surveys thus proceeded independently from the Pacific Ocean east to the summit of the Rockies.

It was not until the fourth year of the Boundary Survey, in the fall of 1860, that the American party reached the Continental Divide in present-day Glacier Park. It was here that James Alden, the official artist of the survey, painted a view to the west along the path over which they had toiled for so long. He then turned around, and painted a scene looking east across Cameron Lake. Heavy snow began falling just as he completed his last sketch of the magnificent mountain landscape.

The British party under Colonel Hawkins reached the highest elevation point of the survey, atop the Continental Divide, in 1861. The Divide intersects the 49th Parallel at an elevation of about 7,300 feet. Upon reaching the long-sought goal, the veterinary surgeon of the expedition, John Keast Lord, joyfully wrote, "wild and beautiful is the scenery on every side, right and left stupendous pinnacle-like hills, white with snow, seem to reach to the clouds; ridge follows ridge, each seeming to be more craggy and massive than its fellow ..."

In March 1872, President Ulysses S. Grant signed the bill authorizing the rest of the survey, from Lake of the Woods, Minnesota, westward to the Continental Divide along the 49th Parallel. In 1874 the survey parties reached the summit of the Rockies, connecting with the point reached by the surveys of 1860 and 1861. The U.S. crew that surveyed up to the Divide was led by a Captain Ames of the Sixth Infantry. They camped on Waterton Lake for some time, mapping the peaks and drainages in the area. Because of a cartographic error in the Pacific Railroad Survey, they called Waterton Lake, "Chief Mountain Lake," a name which actually belonged to Lower St. Mary Lake.

William F. Raynolds

As an Army explorer, Raynolds led an expedition in 1859 into the Yellowstone region to assess the Indian situation, the climate, and the natural resources of the area. He was also to investigate four possible wagon routes, including one from the source of the Wind River in Wyoming to the source of the Missouri River. In June 1860 Raynolds and his party crossed the Continental Divide pass that now bears his name, between the Centennial and Henry's Lake mountain ranges. Floundering through deep snow on the south side of the current Yellowstone Park, Raynolds was unable to verify the "marvelous tales of burning plains, immense lakes, and boiling springs." It would be more than a decade before his surgeon-naturalist, Ferdinand Hayden, would lead the first fully-staffed scientific expedition into this legendary land.

"Slippery Bill" Morrison in his later years near Summit at Marias Pass—a genuine character of the Continental Divide. GLACIER NATIONAL PARK ARCHIVES

William H. "Slippery Bill" Morrison

There are countless tales, some taller than the Great Divide itself, of events that have occurred along the mountain barrier either because of or in spite of their geographic setting. Without doubt, the best of these stories were never recorded, having been lost in obscurity from campfire to campfire over the years. Here is one that was written down, which is worth repeating.

One of the most colorful rangers ever to work for the Forest Service was William Morrison, better known as "Slippery Bill." He provided his own headquarters at Marias Pass and was responsible for the Middle Fork of the Flathead drainage. He held a squatter's right at Summit long before the railroad appeared. When he learned that the Great Northern was coming through the pass, he installed a rosewood bar in his shack and did a flourishing business.

He owned the saloon while he still was appointed ranger. In order to do both jobs, he would stand in the door of his saloon, gaze at the distant landscape, and then write in his government diary, "Looking over the Forest." Slippery Bill's stint with the Forest Service was brief. He spent most of his life trapping, prospecting and living by his wits. His nickname was the result of his astuteness during a poker game at the wild railroad construction camp of McCarthyville. Bill had won heavily, but he knew that he would likely be murdered if he tried to leave with so much money. Pocketing most of his money and leaving a small sum at his place at the card table, he excused himself, saying that he would return in a few minutes. Once outside, he hurried away, thus earning the title, "Slippery Bill." According to Bill, the the melting snows of McCarthyville revealed nine corpses the following spring.

For years Slippery Bill avoided paying taxes on his saloon. When Flathead County officials appeared he claimed that he was located in what was then Teton County. When the Teton officials called on him he told them that his saloon was in Flathead County. The time came when Bill had to make a choice. It seems hat the officials from both counties arrived at the same time.

During the dedication of the Stevens statue at Summit in 1926, John F. Stevens explained how he had nearly perished in a blizzard at the pass. At this point, Morrison spoke up from the crowd, "Why didn't you come over to my house? I was living right over there," as he pointed to his cabin.

Late in life, as a tall, stately old man, Morrison became well known as a rustic philosopher. At the Summit depot, an eastern woman came up to old Bill and asked, "How do people make a living in this unpleasant, wind-swept, God-forsaken place?" Bill replied, "Lady, most of us make a comfortable living by minding our own business."

Morrison agreed to donate the land for building a monument to Theodore Roosevelt at Marias Pass. He stipulated that no concessions, "hamburger stands" as he called them, would be built on any of this property during his lifetime. The 60-foot-high Roosevelt Memorial Obelisk was erected in 1931. Eleanor Roosevelt placed a small, sealed copper box in the cornerstone and covered it with cement. The box contained the appropriations bill for the monument and some other documents.

Slippery Bill passed away in March 1932 at the age of 84. During the summer of that year the Forest Service placed a large boulder on a concrete slab just south of the obelisk as a memorial to William H. Morrison — a genuine character of the Continental Divide.

A Sampler of Ghost Towns and Mining Camps Along the Divide

Altyn — As soon as the Blackfeet legally relinquished their claim to the Ceded Strip in 1895, a hoard of miners rushed back to their previously staked claims to develop their prospects in the Swiftcurrent Mining District of today's Glacier Park.

The mining settlement of Altyn sprang up near Swiftcurrent Lake, and by 1899 the camp boasted two saloons. A wagon road was built from Babb to Altyn and extended six miles up Canyon Creek to Cracker Lake. Records also show that a trail was constructed over the Divide at Swiftcurrent Pass to Granite Park so that pack trains could deliver supplies to the area mines.

By 1900 Altyn had a newspaper, the *Swift Current Courier*. The first issue proclaimed:

COPPER IS KING
NO DOUBT ABOUT THE PERMANENCY AND
PRODUCTIVENESS OF THE
SWIFT CURRENT MINES
NO STOCK FOR SALE.

At the time, local opinion was equally divided that Altyn would either become the richest and biggest camp on earth, or nothing. Today, Altyn is most certainly nothing, having been inundated long ago by Lake Sherburne when a dam was built across Swiftcurrent River.

McCarthyville — once reputed to be the "toughest town in the world," its 18-month existence was spawned by the construction of the Great Northern Railway's mainline across Marias Pass in 1890-1891.

In the spring of 1890 Eugene McCarthy crossed the Divide at Marias Pass and camped at the site of McCarthyville, currently the location of the Bear Creek Ranch, a few miles west of the pass. It was the only flat land near the summit for miles and McCarthy realized that it would be a good spot for the supply camp that railroad construction crews would require.

The town was platted that September and the plats filed in the courthouse at Missoula. At the time, state law prohibited selling liquor within two miles of a construction camp except within an incorporated city. So McCarthy incorporated. Soon after, he was elected mayor at the age of 20.

During its heyday, McCarthyville could be reached only over the steep "tote" road that was built by the railroad as a

Above: *The Swiftcurrent Mining Camp at Altyn in Glacier Park, August 26, 1900. Those who predicted that Altyn would either become the richest mining camp in the world or nothing were right. Today it is nothing.*
Right: *Red Mountain guards the partially occupied mining ghost town of Rimini just east of the Divide near Helena.*
MONTANA HISTORICAL SOCIETY PHOTOS

supply route. Wagons actually had to be lowered down tortuous grades with ropes tied around trees.

Labor was scarce, so the railroad brought laborers from the eastern cities by train to the Cut Bank terminus. From there they had to hike 60 miles over the Divide. During winter, the emigrants frequently were caught by blizzards on the flats and stumbled into town with pneumonia. Mayor McCarthy recalled that the town doctor had come from Great Falls "where we understood he had a fine reputation as a veterinarian." He began to notice that there were not many survivors among the pneumonia patients. "It got so every morning just at daylight a big Swede, a kind of nurse at the hospital, would come outside with a body on a sled wrapped up in a two dollar blanket. After digging a hole in the snow up the creek, he'd roll the corpse off the sled," remembered the mayor.

McCarthy's partner resolved one day to "kill that Swede; he's getting on my nerves with his everlasting funerals at daylight." "No," said the mayor, "the doctor's our man." Apparently, the doctor's contract with the railway company to care for employees for $1 per man per month was not much incentive, as the men were dying before they could get on the payroll. The mayor organized a committee to go after the doctor, but the latter narrowly escaped and "McCarthyville never saw him again."

After the rails were laid past the town the construction headquarters were moved farther west. McCarthyville died as suddenly as it was born.

Mike Horse — this historic mine is located in the headwaters of the Blackfoot River just south of Rogers Pass and only about 1½ miles west of the Continental Divide. It was discovered in 1898 by J.P. Hartmiller when his horse, Old Mike, stumbled and turned over a chunk of rock later found to be lead and copper ore. Upon digging at the spot, Hartmiller uncovered the vein that was still a heavy producer in 1948.

In the 1920s considerable high-grade lead-silver ore was hauled by six-horse teams over Flesher Pass and then by rail to the East Helena smelter.

After Highway 200 was completed east-northeast from Rogers Pass in 1946-1948, the new road was used by the miners to haul concentrates to Helena via Wolf Creek when heavy snow closed 6,350' Flesher Pass in 1948. (Highway 200 west from Rogers Pass would be completed nine years later.) At that time the short-lived town of Mike Horse existed at the mine, with a population of 200 and boasting a school and recreation center.

Gould — located about four miles east of the Continental Divide below Stemple Pass, Gould had a population of 300 in the 1890s but is now an almost nonexistent ghost town.

Well preserved a century after its heyday, Marysville lies nestled in the gold-rich hills of the Continental Divide northwest of Helena. Thomas Cruse, who developed the famed Drumlummon Mine, named the town for Mary Ralston, the first white woman to arrive. BILL CUNNINGHAM

The Jay Gould, one of the largest mines in the district, was discovered in 1884 and was worked intermittently until the mid-1930s.

Long before legal prohibition came to Montana (1919), Gould is believed to have been the first place in Montana that went dry and the only place never to have its thirst slaked again. In the 1890s the manager of the Jay Gould Mine, Owen Byrnes, declared, "The saloons must go; too many miners are drinking before going on shift and then getting killed in the mines." Byrnes promptly bought one of the two saloons in town and closed it. The other saloon keeper refused to sell, so his watering hole was acquired more creatively through a rigged horse race. And that is how "real" prohibition first came to Montana.

Byrnes built a power plant on the Landers Fork of the Big Blackfoot River to service his mines. The dam held but the water in the reservoir leaked out through fissures in the rock. Byrnes also had failed to allow for contraction and expansion on his power line to Gould and, during the first winter, the wires snapped between every pole.

Penobscot Mine — the remnants of this historic mine are located three miles above Marysville, precisely on top of the Continental Divide. Today, the sad remains of a mine that once produced more than $1 million worth of gold consist only of two mine shafts, surrounded by chain-link fences with warning signs that announce a mine reclamation site.

The Penobscot was discovered in 1874 and purchased in 1876 by Nate Vestal. Vestal built an arrastra (a primitive mill) and began working the mine dumps. The richness of the waste ore convinced him to go ahead with active mining. Soon he was deeply in debt, but his personal magnetism convinced his unpaid miners to stick with him. Their faith paid off with one of the biggest Montana gold strikes to date. Ore averaged $1,000 per foot in the first 50 feet of the shaft.

Vestal was a natural public-relations man, arranging tours of the mine and displaying a 242-pound gold bar worth $54,262.62 at a Helena bank to attract investors. He eventually sold the mine for $350,000 and used some of the proceeds to finance an unknown miner, Thomas Cruse, to develop the unknown Drumlummon Mine — a fabulously successful venture that caused the near-ghost town of Marysville to attain a population of 5,000 in the early 1890s.

In 1940 writer T.J. Kertulla summarized the history of the Penobscot as " ... the mine of the day, and its history is the story of practically every other gold mine in the country, large or small ... the Helena newspapers were loud and persistent in their efforts to convince all comers that it was the greatest gold mine in the world. Perhaps it was, but later gold and silver discoveries so much richer have pushed it back into obscurity. Even those who live close by have forgotten its story. Such is fame."

Today, little remains of Blackfoot City—one of Montana's first mining boom towns just west of the Divide near Avon. The town cemetery sits on a hill above the old townsite with several undated tombstones that are likely of 1860s vintage. MONTANA HISTORICAL SOCIETY

Red Mountain City and **Highland City** — were two adjacent mining settlements on the Continental Divide in the Highland Mountains directly south of Butte. By the summer of 1867 the camps were the largest settlement in southern Deer Lodge County, which at that time reached from the Highlands north to Canada.

The sick were treated by Dr. Seymour Day whenever he was sober. During the winter of 1867 a "grand ball" was held after a heavy snow had closed the road for two days before the event. Two hundred men dug out six miles of snow-packed road so that all could attend.

Several of those men working placer claims built long flumes to bring additional water to their properties. Since the entire district was on the crest of the Divide, above 7,000 feet, the streams were frozen under deep snows for several months each year.

By 1874 both camps were virtually deserted. For many years the only resident was an oldtimer, John Kern, who arrived there by wagon in 1866 and died there in 1923. He worked his placer claim and cared for the grave of his girlfriend, a dancehall girl called "Shotgun Liz" who died in 1867. Liz earned the nickname by shooting a man who was molesting her.

The most important later mine was the Butte Highland property on Basin Creek, three miles west of Highland City. Its 100-ton cyanide mill had to be rebuilt in 1932 on the Moose Creek (east) side of the Divide so as not to pollute Butte's water system. Both mine and mill shut down in 1942.

French Gulch — located on the east side of the Divide about 15 miles south of Anaconda, the first discovery was made by a Frenchman in the fall of 1864. The gulch was worked continuously for either gold mining or logging until the late 1920s.

The key player in French Gulch was William Allen, born there in 1871, a Montana Congressman. Copper baron Marcus Daly bought the French Gulch Dredging Company and he and Allen extended an 18-mile flume for logging from French Gulch, over the Continental Divide, to the railroad junction on Mill Creek. For eight years around the turn of the century, from 1,800 to 2,500 poles per day were flumed over the Divide at an elevation of 6,600' for shipment to the Butte mines. At the time this early logging was under Forest Service supervision — one of the first such timber sales in the nation and a training ground for forestry students.

Blackfoot City (Ophir) — was located May 16, 1865, on Ophir Gulch a few miles west of the Continental Divide north of Avon. Copper baron William A. Clark is said to have made his start here teaching school.

On June 28, 1865, several of the town fathers were attacked and killed by Indians who resented the white men taking too much timber and wild game.

In 1867 A.K. McClure visited Blackfoot City as part of his 3,000-mile Rocky Mountain tour and had this to say about the mining camp: "Half the cabins are groggeries, about one-fifth are gambling saloons, and a large percentage are occupied by the fair but frail ones who ever follow miner's camp ... I stood on a box in front of the hotel, with a bar doing a brisk business behind me ... on my left, with double doors and windows open, was a gambling saloon, in full blast, with a faro-bank, three or four poker tables, a billiard table, a bar, all liberally patronized ... I left the famous city of Blackfoot with few regrets. A Sunday there is anything but pleasant to one who don't gamble, race horses, or buy at street-auctions."

As many as 500 Chinese were working the Blackfoot City mines, and one of them ran a grocery store. Large shipments of rice were received from China and hauled over the Divide by ox-team. The teams forded the Little Blackfoot River at Avon. Once during high water the rice in three wagons became well soaked. By the time it reached Blackfoot City the rice had swollen and burst out of the straw sacks.

Above: *Butte, surrounded on three sides by the Continental Divide with the Divide in the background to the east, in 1890.* HAYNES FOUND. COLL., MONTANA HISTORICAL SOCIETY

Far left: *Montana's future territorial capital of Bannack had only 400 to 500 residents when the east-side mining camp of French Gulch near Anaconda was beginning to take shape on August 23, 1862.* MONTANA HISTORICAL SOCIETY

Left: *The story of this dilapidated waterwheel below Carp Creek near the crest of the Anaconda-Pintlers has been lost in obscurity.* COURTESY, U.S. FOREST SERVICE

Rails and Roads Across the Divide

Pacific Railroad Surveys

Through the 1840s, as pressure for a transcontinental railroad built, some in Congress still doubted its feasibility. One Congressman loudly proclaimed that the "Rockies were purposely created as a barrier for all time between the East and the West."

Despite such convincing rhetoric, in 1853 Congress ordered the Secretary of War, Jefferson Davis, to report on all practicable routes between the Canadian and Mexican borders for a transcontinental railroad. Davis appointed Isaac Stevens to direct the survey of the northern tier. Stevens was governor of Washington Territory, which at that time included what is now Montana west of the Continental Divide.

The governor knew, in a general way, of the existence of Marias Pass from an 1840 map published by Robert Greenhow, which showed almost the exact location of the pass, labeled "Route across the Mountains." This was the earliest published record of the existence of the pass.

Stevens was visited in Fort Benton by Little Dog, a Piegan chief, who accurately described Marias Pass as "a broad, wide, open valley with scarcely a hill or obstruction on this road excepting here and there some fallen timber."

In late September 1853 the governor crossed the Blackfoot Pass on the Divide at the suggestion of his hunter, a French-Canadian-Indian mixed-blood named Pierre Cadotte, who had used it while trapping in 1851. From then on the defile was known as Cadotte Pass (6,044'), which is just south of Lewis and Clark Pass on the same Dearborn and Blackfoot River drainages.

About the crossing, Stevens wrote, "As we ascended the divide, a severe pelting hail and rain storm, accompanied with high wind, thunder, and lightning, came upon us and did not abate until we had reached the summit ... It was with great gratification that we now left the plains of the Missouri to enter upon the country watered by the Columbia ... I was a good deal surprised to find how small an obstacle this divide was to the movement of a wagon-train."

At this open top of the Continental Divide, the governor issued a proclamation announcing the existence of the new Washington Territory and establishing its civil government, which was himself.

Just having crossed the once-elusive summit of Marias Pass, this Great Northern Railway train begins its westward descent along the Middle Fork of the Flathead River. MONTANA HISTORICAL SOCIETY

The elusive Marias Pass continued to be a frustration as several attempts by the Stevens survey failed to locate it. A final effort for 1853 was made when Stevens sent one of his engineers, Abiel Tinkham, to find the pass from the west. Tinkham crossed the Divide at 7,600' and rapidly descended 2,000' to the head of one of the tributaries of the Marias. He had crossed Cut Bank Pass in Glacier Park, the first white man known to do so since 1810, when an employee of David Thompson named MacDonald travelled the route.

In January 1854, Lt. Cuvier Grover of the Stevens party left Fort Benton for Cadotte Pass with four dogsleds. He was not hindered by snow, but by the lack of it, so he waited for a snowstorm that would permit him to travel. The dogs were followed by wolves, which would eat the dogsled harnesses at night. As his party crossed the pass the mercury dipped to 38 below, and Grover complained, "sometimes I had my mouth frozen open, and sometimes shut, according to the position it happened to be kept in for half an hour."

In the spring of 1854, Stevens sent James Doty to find Marias Pass. After exploring several valleys he moved up one of the forks of the Two Medicine near present-day East Glacier. From a nearby hill, he could see the southwest course of Marias Pass, a dozen or so miles toward a low portion of the Continental Divide. Seen but not explored was the location of Marias Pass, which he merely deemed "worthy of further examination." That "further examination" would be a long time coming.

All told, Stevens and his men explored nine Continental Divide passes. In the end, Stevens advocated a railroad route over Cadotte Pass, overlooking such details as the steep grades approaching the pass, the severe climate, and the heavy snowfall in the area. He was eventually overruled, and the first transcontinental railroad, completed in 1869, utilized South Pass in Wyoming.

In 1855 Stevens helped negotiate treaties with some of the western Indian tribes. Stevens convinced the Kalispel, Flathead, and Kutenai tribes to form a confederation — now known as the Confederated Salish and Kootenai Tribes — and to accept a reservation in the Flathead Lake area. In return, the Indians gave up their aboriginal claims to the northern passes, thereby making possible the transcontinental railroad.

John F. Stevens

Great Northern Railway developer James J. Hill was determined that his line would cross the Continental Divide's formidable barrier by the lowest, most direct route — through the fabled Marias Pass that Chief Little Dog had described to Isaac Stevens more than 30 years earlier.

Hill placed John F. Stevens in charge of the mountain reconnaissance in 1889. It was already late November, and a bitter, bone-chilling cold and heavy snow covered the crest of the mountains. At the Badger Creek Blackfeet Agency, Stevens convinced a reluctant Flathead Indian called Coonsah to accompany him to the pass. Coonsah was wanted for murder on the Flathead Reservation, so his reluctance was understandable.

Soon the two were traveling up Two Medicine Creek on improvised snowshoes. When they reached False Summit, east of the actual Marias Pass, the Flathead announced that he was unable to proceed in the bitter cold, so Stevens forged on alone.

At last Stevens came to the source of the stream he had been following. Had he found the real Marias Pass? Trembling with excitement, he checked his barometer, which read barely 5,000 feet above sea level. To make certain, he slogged west until he found another stream (Bear Creek) flowing west toward the Pacific. He had found it!

Right: *The east approach to the Mullan Tunnel underneath the Continental Divide, which provided Montana's first trans-Divide railway service in 1883.* HAYNES FOUND. COLL., MONTANA HISTORICAL SOCIETY
Far right: *The Milwaukee Road crosses the Divide at Pipestone Pass just east of Butte.* MONTANA HISTORICAL SOCIETY

The cold, exhausted railroad engineer was forced to bivouac for the night at the summit in a deep freeze of 40 below zero. He stayed alive by walking back and forth in a track about 100 yards long. "One advantage of the extreme cold," Stevens remarked, "was that mosquitoes didn't bother me." The next morning, he found the sleeping Coonsah half frozen, but alive. They were both able to struggle down the rest of the 1,500' pass to the Indian agency.

The rediscovery of Marias by Stevens gave the Great Northern a route to the west coast that was 100 miles shorter than the other lines' routes. The steel reached the summit of the Continental Divide on September 14, 1891. In 1893 the first Great Northern transcontinental train rumbled over the lowest railway pass across the Divide north of Mexico.

Certainly a highlight in Stevens' life occurred on July 21, 1926, when a special ceremony was held at Marias Pass. A 12-foot-high bronze statue of John Stevens was unveiled in recognition of his rediscovery of Marias Pass on December 11, 1889. The modest Stevens commented that all it took was a strong man to carry it out, but that he was pretty strong in those days. (At the current writing, the Stevens statue is being restored at sculptor Bob Scriver's Browning studio.)

Northern Pacific Railroad

The central question in reaching the Pacific was how best to carry the road over the main Divide of the Rocky Mountains. During the preliminary surveys of 1871 and 1872 Chief Engineer Milnor Roberts had studied 15 passes over the Continental Divide. He then eliminated all but Deer Lodge, Pipestone and Mullan. Roberts favored Deer Lodge as it had easy approaches and no tunnel, but this route was longer. Pipestone had the highest summit of the three, with the worst approaches. Mullan Pass gave the shortest line, but required a long tunnel.

Roberts' successor, General Adna Anderson, changed the location to Mullan Pass. Construction for the tunnel began on December 14, 1881. Instead of being solid with good support, the rock was highly fractured with a great deal of limestone. Extensive log supports were needed, so that the combination of bad rock and logging the adjacent slopes delayed the completion of the 3,850' tunnel. The elevation of the Mullan tunnel is 5,547', with the highest point being on the west side. The elevation of the Divide at Mullan Pass is 5,902'.

When the first passenger train crossed the Continental Divide at Mullan Pass in 1883 it was met in Garrison by a party including railway officials, former president Ulysses S. Grant and Sitting Bull. The last passenger train rumbled over the pass on May 31, 1971.

Now, the trains that cross the Divide daily are hauling some 9,000 tons of freight and are pushed by three 3,000-horsepower diesel engines. The 10-mile, 2.2-percent grade over Mullan Pass is the longest stretch of mountain grade on the entire Burlington Northern line. There are more than 20 curves along a 40-minute haul that uses more than 200 of the 300 gallons of fuel needed for the total run between Helena and Missoula.

Every engineer who ever hauled the pass has in the back of his mind an awareness that the engine might slip on the track. If that were to happen, the coupling knuckle could break and the diesel could pull the train apart — something the old steam engines could not do.

Milwaukee Road

The main line was opened for through freight service in July 1909. It climbed the east summit of the Continental Divide at Donald, the east entrance to the 2,290-foot-long Pipestone Pass tunnel. The line seemed steeper than it really was with 21 miles of 2 percent grade and numerous curves right on the edge of the mountains. The road west descends a 1 percent grade through the tunnel and a 1.66 percent grade for 10 miles into Butte.

Because of the disappointing performance of steam power on the mountain grades, the decision was made to electrify the 113-mile stretch of rail from Deer Lodge, over the Continental Divide, to Three Forks. On November 24, 1914, the first contract for 42 locomotives and equipment was signed. One year later, on November 30, 1915, the trolley wire was energized for the first time between Butte and the Eustis substation at the foot of the grade on the east side of the Divide. On that same morning, locomotive #10200 ran west across the Continental Divide to Butte. Proclaimed "the largest electric locomotive in the world," #10200 had left Chicago on October 6 for an exhibition tour along the line to Tacoma.

Above: *With the majesty of Glacier Park as a backdrop, the Great Northern crosses the Divide at Marias Pass in 1964.* MONTANA HISTORICAL SOCIETY Below: *The first train into Rimini, just east of the Divide, consisted of Northern Pacific locomotive No. 102 and a caboose.* HAYNES FOUND. COLL., MONTANA HISTORICAL SOCIETY

The Saga of Cromwell Dixon: The First Heavier than Air Flight over the Continental Divide

Over the years there have been many "firsts" associated with Montana's stretch of the Continental Divide: the first road across, the first railroad crossing, the first exploration by a white explorer, the first stagecoach, the first Masonic meeting, the first cattle drive, the first escape from the law, the first of almost anything you can imagine. Most of these stirring but often unrecorded events have been forever obscured with the passage of time. But one such "first" stands out with such drama and excitement that not only was it vividly recorded at the time, but it also continues to capture the imagination: the first airplane flight over the nation's Great Divide, just west of Helena in 1911.

The star attraction at the 1911 Montana State Fair was a daily exhibition flight by a daring 19-year-old pilot named Cromwell Dixon from Columbus, Ohio. Dixon had purchased his airplane from the Curtiss Exhibition Company of New York City. He was paying for the machine by doing exhibition flights booked by the Curtiss Company.

There was a high degree of excitement in the air on the morning of September 30 as Helena buzzed with the word that Dixon was going to attempt the first flight ever over the Continental Divide. Impossible, said the skeptics. Indeed, there was every reason to doubt that the youthful aviator could accomplish the task. After all, his flimsy craft was nothing more than a two-winged kite with an engine attached precariously between the wings. The wing struts were fashioned from bamboo, with young Dixon perched out front in an open seat. But the pilot's tender years belied the more than five years of flying experience he had under his belt — enough experience to rank him as one of the first 50 pilots in the nation to receive a license.

The State Fair was to climax on September 30 with Cromwell Dixon flying from the Helena fairgrounds, across the Divide near Mullan Pass to the town of Blossburg, and returning to the fairgrounds. If successful, Dixon stood to win a purse of $10,000 put up by local aviation enthusiasts.

The historic flight was preceded by extensive preparations. An automobile was sent to Blossburg with a mechanic and a can of gasoline. A huge bonfire, Dixon's beacon light, was kindled on top of the Divide and the word was sent to Blossburg and Austin that the flight was about to begin. The young pilot prepared for the event by wearing heavier clothes than usual, including a woolen aviator's cap that encased his head and face. The course of the flight was to lead due west to a hill beyond Fort Harrison and from there a few degrees north of west, over the town of Austin, and then in a direct line over the bonfire atop the Divide a mile north of Blossburg.

At exactly 2 p.m. the smiling lad of 19 took off in his motor kite, heading due north after circling the fairgrounds. Upon gaining 3,000 feet he swung west toward the Divide. Dixon clutched the control stick as his tiny craft climbed into the sun. His face was chilled by the mountain winds that seemed to add lift to his flight. Soon he spotted Blossburg and the crowd below. Just 34 minutes after he had taken off Dixon made history by crossing the Continental Divide at 7,000 feet and landing on a grassy slope one-half mile from the little community near Mullan Pass.

Dixon presented the dignitaries at Blossburg with a letter from Governor Edwin L. Norris, thanking them for their cooperation. He then sent a telegram from Blossburg's railroad depot to the Curtiss Exhibition Company in New York advising of his achievement.

At 3:16 p.m. the first trans-Divide aviator took off down the sloping field and was sighted crossing the Continental Divide at 3:37 p.m. During his return flight Dixon encountered the ordeal of 30 m.p.h. gusts of wind with tricky crosscurrents. After a near-fatal brush with the main range of the Rocky Mountains, Dixon nursed his craft out of a mountain basin and arrived at the Helena fairgrounds a short time later.

Cromwell Dixon was given a hero's ovation by the record fair crowd. The throng demanded a speech but the bashful youth could only blush. Governor Norris, in the true spirit of Montana politicians, rose to the occasion and proclaimed Dixon the greatest aviator in the world.

Dixon had won the hearts of Montanans, but tragedy struck only two days later when the young aviator plunged to his death during a fair exhibition flight at Spokane. Headlines in Helena read, "Dixon Falls to Death — City of Helena in Tears — Youthful Aviator Crashes to Ground When Gust of Wind Catches Machine in Spokane."

In 1939 the U.S. Forest Service dedicated a campground and picnic area atop the Continental Divide at MacDonald Pass as "Camp Cromwell Dixon." Located 15 miles west of Montana's capital city, the popular campground was

Top: *Cromwell Dixon prepares, near Blossburg, for his return flight over the Divide.*
Left: *Dixon circles the fairgrounds before heading toward the Continental Divide.*
Above: *The star attraction at the 1911 Montana State Fair, Cromwell Dixon.* MONTANA HISTORICAL SOCIETY PHOTOS

described by the Helena paper as " ... one of the finest outdoor camping spots in the west, within an easy hour's drive of Helena."

Lamenting the untimely death of the brave young pilot the October 3, 1911, edition of the (Helena) *Montana Record* had this to say: "And it was only last Saturday that he soared over the grandstand on his return flight from his world's record over the continental divide, his face flushed with embarrassed modesty as the big crowd cheered, and a broad, boyish smile of triumph on his countenance! Now he is dead.

"Mourned in Helena is this child; he was scarcely more than that. Some mourn for the daredevil that he was; but the majority mourn for the boy that has gone. The men liked him because he was unspoiled; mothers liked him because he reminded them of their own sons; boys liked him because he was a boy the instant he left the machine; and the girls liked him, because he was gallant."

Above: *"Now you see it, now you don't" as a slice of hillside just east of MacDonald Pass makes way for the new highway more than a half century ago.* MONTANA HISTORICAL SOCIETY ARCHIVES

It took a determination to match the awesome terrain and snow depths of the Great Divide itself finally to build Going-to-the-Sun Highway over Glacier Park's Logan Pass. MONTANA HISTORICAL SOCIETY

Highways and Byways Across the Great Divide

The first engineered road to bisect Montana's Continental Divide was the historic one built by John Mullan over the pass that bears his name. Then came the steel rails and the belching iron horses. With the advent of the horseless carriage the demand skyrocketed for roads that would link east with west over the Great Divide. Most of these transmountain roadways were first constructed in the early part of this century. In many cases, a sort of natural evolution occurred: game and Indian trails, explorer routes, wagon roads, a pair of rutted vehicle tracks, single-lane roads without and later with pavement, and now, in a few cases, modern four-lane Interstate highways. As with rails, the key question with each road was how to cross the imposing dividing ridge of the Rockies. Here is part of the

story about two of the approximately 20 paved and unpaved roadways that cut across the Divide in Montana.

Going-to-the-Sun Highway Across Logan Pass in Glacier Park

By 1914 a road finally had reached the park's eastern border, but an automobile could continue west in only two ways — by loading the vehicle onto a Great Northern flatcar for shipment to Belton (West Glacier) or by a lengthy detour to the closest road crossing the Divide near Helena. Both options involved a cost and inconvenience that few motorists wanted to endure.

The growing pressure for a road transecting the Park that would unite its isolated east and west sides was bluntly expressed by P.N. Bernard, Secretary of the Kalispell Chamber of Commerce: "A Park without roads is a menace to civilization and settlement and a barrier to communication between states and districts."

At first the route was proposed over the difficult Gunsight Pass, which even its advocate, Park Service engineer Lyman Sperry, conceded would require "a number of interesting — but not forbidding — 'stunts' in engineering and autoing." Later, a reconnaissance survey by engineer George Goodwin revealed that a road over Logan Pass could be built more easily than any other route investigated. The pass was named after Major W.R. Logan, the first superintendent of Glacier Park. He was the son of a renowned Indian fighter, Capt. William Logan, who was killed in 1877 at the Battle of the Big Hole.

By the summer of 1924 work progressing on the transmountain road on both sides of the Park was approaching its most difficult phase — the crossing of the awesome escarpment of the Continental Divide through Logan Pass. In September of that year a reconnaissance of the best route to the pass began. It was barely accomplished when four feet of snow fell on November 5. Many men broke under the strain in the rush to finish the survey before winter. In order to keep 32 men on the job

Left: *Wisdom, Montana, 1900. The stageline ran from Divide, Montana, through Wisdom, over the Continental Divide at Big Hole Pass, and on into Gibbonsville, Idaho. The stage left Divide at 6 p.m. daily, arriving at Gibbonsville at 8 a.m. the following day.*
Right: *Gone are the stately portal and towering lodgepole pines that decorated Gibbons Pass shortly after the Bitterroot-Big Hole road was opened in 1914.*

continuously, 135 were employed. The survey leader observed that "there were really three crews: one coming, one working and one going." The following year the survey crew had to hang from cliffs on ropes to take cross-sections. Three workers died while working on the road, two from falls and one from a falling rock.

On July 15, 1933, the Going-to-the-Sun road was opened to public travel and dedication ceremonies were conducted at Logan Pass. A crowd of more than 4,000 gathered to celebrate the culmination of more than 20 years of planning, anticipation and construction. The Director of the National Park Service, Horace Albright, restated the firm policy of the first Park Service Director, Stephen T. Mather: Let there be no completion of other roads across the Park. Going-to-the-Sun Highway should stand supreme and alone.

The Bitterroot-Big Hole Road Across Gibbons Pass

In order to descend the steep grade of the Big Hole wagon road, built in 1878, wagons would stop on top to chain a small tree behind to serve as a brake. During the 1880s and 1890s trees were scattered all over the foot of the mountain.

In 1914 the 26-mile-long Big Hole Road was built on the old Gibbons Trail from Camp Creek, over Gibbons Pass, and down Trail Creek to the Big Hole Battlefield at a cost of $52,000. As recorded in the *Western News* of Hamilton, as the road neared completion, people became aware that Darby and Wisdom were about to be united. The Wisdom Chamber of Commerce invited Bitterrooters to send a pilot car over the new road for a gala celebration in the Big Hole. Dr. Herbert Hayward and Al Rissman, staunch supporters of the road, accepted the offer since Dr. Hayward owned a brand new Ford runabout.

Thus, in September, they lashed two planks on each side of the car (for use in fording streams) and started out with Wisdom ready to celebrate the arrival of the intrepid motorists. It was not long before the car's radiator began boiling over. The two Darby men repeatedly climbed down the mountain for water until they became exhausted. They then spent considerable time allowing the red-hot engine to cool after short climbs. It was almost dusk when the trail blazers topped the summit where the road camp was located. There they hit a stump, which tore out the oil plug. The camp blacksmith fashioned a wooden plug, replaced

the lost oil with cottalene, and they headed down Trail Creek in the dark.

A couple of miles farther, they entered a large prairie where they hit a rock that bent the car's wishbone. After spending a cold, sleepless night in an old log cabin, they managed to pound the wishbone back into shape, replace it, and steer the auto down the road. Again and again they crossed the creek until the car slipped off the planks at Ruby Creek and mired down.

Luckily, a cowboy came along and affixed his lasso to the bumper. They started the engine, the horse bolted, and the cowboy was left in the mud. The three men walked to the Ruby Ranch, where they secured another horse and eventually pulled the car to dry ground.

Soon they were on the home stretch to Wisdom, 15 miles away, where they found the celebration worn off, the steaks cold, and the celebrators somewhat the worse for wear in the town saloon healing their wounds. Editor Dick Hathaway of the *Big Hole Breezes*, wearing a 20-gallon hat and filled to the gills with moose milk, positioned the Bitterrooters on top of the bar where they were toasted repeatedly until everyone felt fine again. After some car and other repair of a personal nature, the Darby motorists made it clear back to Darby in a single day.

Continental Divide Place Names

The origins of many of the hundreds of place names along Montana's Great Divide have never been recorded. If we could determine the exact circumstances and derivation of each place name, we would have an almost complete history of the exploration, development and settlement of the Divide region. Names give us fascinating glimpses of the ethnic origin of the people who took possession of the country, their occupation, events in their lives, in short, a sort of geographical celebration of both the great and the obscure.

The first significant geographic record of Montana came as a result of the Lewis and Clark Expedition of 1804-1806. Close on the heels of Lewis and Clark came the romantic and adventurous era of the fur trade. Within 30 years the pelt hunters had traversed most hidden streams and valleys along the Divide. Each of the major streams, mountains and ranges was quickly named. The names were passed among the trappers by word of mouth until they could be perpetuated on maps. And many of those names were no doubt lost before they could be entered on maps.

There are surprisingly few Indian place names in Montana. "Montana" itself is derived from the Spanish, or perhaps directly from the Latin, meaning mountainous. Ohio congressman James M. Ashley applied it to Montana Territory; he obviously liked the name for a Rocky Mountain locale — the year before, he had tried to have Idaho Territory called Montana when it was created.

Roberta Carkeek Cheney's *Names on the Face of Montana* has been of assistance in compiling this list of name origins along the Divide.

Alice Creek — named for Alice Cox, who died young; her family homesteaded in the drainage, which is on the southern end of the Scapegoat Wilderness near Lewis and Clark Pass.

Anaconda — a few miles north of the Divide in southwestern Montana, started by copper king Marcus Daly, who personally picked the spot for the smelter serving Butte because it was near ample water and limestone. An adventurous Irish miner, Michael Hickey, had named his Butte silver mine the "Anaconda" after he had read a Horace Greeley editorial in the *New York Tribune* stating that Grant's army was "encircling Lee's forces like a giant anaconda." Daly later acquired the mine,

and kept the name for his giant copper company.

Bloody Dick Creek — has headwaters near the Divide at Goldstone Pass in southwestern Montana; named for an Englishman named Richards who settled on the creek. His favorite adjective was "bloody."

Big Hole (River, Valley, Pass) — A mountain basin named in the tradition of Jackson Hole and Ross Hole, this really is a hole in the earth's crust. See Geology chapter.

Blossburg — Northern Pacific station just west of Mullan Pass near Helena; named by Wicks, a mining engineer, after a Pennsylvania coal mining town. The original name was Mullan, which caused confusion over shipments for Mullan, Idaho.

Butte — Just west of the Divide in southwestern Montana; miners dubbed the mining camp, taking the name from the nearby "sentinel-like peak" of Big Butte (Cheney), which stands 6,369' high.

Centennial (Mountains, Valley) — the valley just north of the Divide and close to Yellowstone Park was named in 1876, in honor of the nation's centennial, by two prominent stockmen of the area. William Orr and Philip Poindexter established the P&O Ranch along Blacktail Creek, which later became the Matador Cattle Company.

Champion Pass — on the Divide between Helena and Butte; named after a mining camp near Deer Lodge.

Chinese Wall — a 13-mile-long limestone escarpment in the heart of the Bob Marshall Wilderness; resembles the Great Wall of China but no one seems to know who named it.

Dearborn River — headwaters on Scapegoat Mountain in the southern end of the Bob Marshall Country; on July 18, 1805, Capt. Meriwether Lewis named "this handsome bold and clear stream ... in honor of the Secretary of War ... "

False Summit — Old-timers say that when engineers were making the original location surveys for the Great Northern Railway they thought this point was the summit of the Continental Divide. They later found the Divide at Marias Pass about six miles to the west.

Flathead River — named for a group of Salish-speaking Indians in the area. The group was called Flathead by other bands of Indians in the mistaken belief that Flatheads pressed the heads of their young to flatten them.

Flat Top Mountain — along the Divide south of Marias Pass; the origin of the name is in doubt since there are no flat tops on the mountain. (Not to be confused with Flat Top Mountain in the middle of Glacier National Park, well north of Marias Pass.) It has quite a colorful past. In 1924 Joe Haley and Mose Gillan got away with about 200 head of sheep belonging to the Northwest Livestock Company. The

rustlers were found hiding atop the mountain. Haley also kept a moonshine still on the mountain. In another incident, the notorious outlaw J.J. Smith was killed on Flat Top resisting arrest.

Flesher Pass — named for Gideon Flesher, the first postmaster at nearby Wilborn in 1902.

Going-to-the-Sun Mountain (Highway) — above Logan Pass in Glacier Park. A myth, perhaps of Blackfeet origin, tells how the Old Man Napi taught the Indians the arts of hunting and agriculture. His mission completed, Napi left for his home in the sun. Climbing a majestic mountain, he disappeared amid swirling snow and flashes of lightning. When the sun burst forth, the Indians saw the chief's profile high on the mountain, engraved in rock and filled with snow.

Gould Creek (Mine) — near Stemple Pass northwest of Helena; named for financier Jay Gould, by Ted Harris, Jack Carpenter and Dick Evans, who discovered gold in the drainage in the early 1880s.

Greenhorn Mountain (Town) — on the Divide just south of Marysville. When the Drumlummon mine was in its heyday an investor in the mine sent his two young sons to Marysville to get some "mining experience." They asked the manager of the mine where to prospect. The manager was quite busy so he arbitrarily pointed to the highest mountain and said, "that mountain is just as good as any place." The boys worked hard and without success all summer, and the mountain became known locally as "Greenhorn." Later, the boys struck paying placer gold on a nearby creek. Greenhorn was also the name of a nearby prosperous mining camp. In April 1883 the territorial Governor of Montana telegraphed postal authorities: "VIGILANTES AT GREENHORN MONTANA HAVE REMOVED POSTMASTER BY HANGING ... OFFICE NOW VACANT" (Cheney).

Hart Creek (Basin) — along Divide in northern Bob Marshall Wilderness; named for Forest Service employee Evert Hart, who built the Limestone and Black Bear cabins in 1925.

Homestake Pass — the ultimate success of a miner was to find enough gold for a "homestake," meaning "he could afford to take his 'stake' and go home to the states from the Montana Territory." (Cheney)

Jackson — in the Big Hole Valley just east of the Divide; named for Anton Jackson, the first postmaster in 1896. (Cheney)

Lima — east of the Divide just north of Monida Pass in southwestern Montana; originally called Allerdice, the name was chosen by early settler Henry Thompson for his home, Lima, Wisconsin. (Cheney)

For two bits a lone horse rider could gain passage over Priest Pass—the site of Valentine Priest's toll house. Today, with the same dirt road in service, the pass is likely crossed by more cattle than people. MONTANA HISTORICAL SOCIETY

Marysville — a famous mining town about 20 miles northwest of Helena just east of the Divide; was one of the state's leading gold producers in the 1880s. Thomas Cruse, who discovered the Drumlummon Mine there, named his strike after his home in Ireland and the town for Mary Ralston, the first white women to arrive. (Cheney)

Pearl Basin — high subalpine basin just east of Camp Creek Pass on the Divide in the southern end of the Bob Marshall Wilderness; named after Pearl Furman. She and her father prospected and camped for some time in this basin in the early 1890s.

Priest Pass — Valentine Priest had come to the Divide country with Jim Bridger in 1864. After 15 years of prospecting, he decided to find a new way across the mountains. Priest operated a toll road across this pass just west of Helena. He charged a dollar for a horse and wagon; $3 for a wagon train; 25 cents for a rider on horseback; and 75 cents for a buggy. In 1883 the Northern Pacific opened its main line across the Divide at nearby Mullan Pass and the whole freighting and travel picture changed.

Red Rock River (Pass, Lakes) — located in southwestern Montana's Centennial Valley; named for the predominantly red rocks in nearby bluffs. (Cheney)

Rimini — old mining town just east of the Divide near Helena; said to be named by Lawrence Barret for the character in the operatic tragedy, "Francisca da Rimini."

Ross Hole — in the upper Bitterroot Valley just west of the Divide; where Alexander Ross and a large brigade of fur trappers camped in March 1823. Ross called it "The Valley of Troubles," because of the hardships in forcing a way through the deep snows along the Divide into the Big Hole Basin.

Scapegoat Mountain — a massive, 9,204' mountain complex along the Divide in the southern end of the Bob Marshall Country; named by a Mr. Chapman of the USGS, who headed a survey party in the area from 1897 to 1900, as the scapegoat on which to blame the group's surveying problems.

Sock Lake — hangs just east of the Divide along the northern Chinese Wall in the Bob Marshall Wilderness. When a fire crew was "mopping up" a nearby forest fire in the 1920s, they found socks dangling from some trees at the lake, hence the name.

Spotted Bear River (Pass) — About 1861, two California miners hired a guide named Baptiste to pack them through the present-day Bob Marshall Wilderness to the east side of the Divide. To avoid the unfriendly Blackfeet, Baptiste decided that the best route would be up the South Fork of the Flathead to the Spotted Bear River, over the Divide and then down the Sun River. While camping near the mouth of the Spotted Bear River, they saw a black bear with an unusual amount of white on its breast and underside. The name "Spotted Bear" has stuck ever since.

Sun River (Pass) — named by sun-worshipping Indians because of the brilliance of the light reflecting from the numerous cliff walls in the upper reaches of the river and from the open, light-buff-colored plains east of the mountains. Plains Indians would gather along the river for the sun dance. It was called Medicine River by Lewis and Clark.

Teton River (Mountain, Pass) — popular opinion has it that the word came from French trappers who commonly attached the word to a mountain; in French, *teton* means "breast." However, there is an Indian tribe belonging to the Sioux Nation called the Teton, who lived along the Missouri River. A report by Major W.A. Powell to the Smithsonian Institution says that "Titon" or "Teton" is from the Indian word "Titan," which means at or on land without trees. The word referred to any of the Indians who lived on the prairie, rather than to a specific tribe.

White River — a major tributary of the South Fork in the heart of the Bob Marshall Wilderness, west of the Divide. The Forest Service named it for western/adventure writer Stewart Edward White, author of the Andy Burnett novels.

Wisdom — in the Big Hole Valley, east of the Divide in southwestern Montana. The journal of Captain Meriwether Lewis reads, "I called the bold rapid and clear stream Wisdom, and the more mild and placid one which flows in from the S.E. Philanthropy, in commemoration of those cardinal virtues, which have so eminently marked that deservedly selibrated character [President Thomas Jefferson] through life." Apparently, these names were too "hifalutin" for the frontiersmen and disappeared. Curiously, the main tributary of the Big Hole River is the Wise River, and the name Wisdom lives on in the Big Hole Basin town.

Wrong Creek — tributary of the Sun River east of the Divide in the Bob Marshall Wilderness, named by government surveyors about 1898. They had thought they were working at the headwaters of the Sun River, but when they realized they were instead on a tributary, they named it Wrong.

(Note: the name origins of many of the Continental Divide passes not listed here are included in the section "Gateways Along the Great Divide.")

Life on the Divide Today

The colorful history of the Sieben Ranch is literally a microcosm of the history of Montana. Henry Sieben walked with a wagon train from Illinois to Montana in 1864 when he was 17. He traveled the Bozeman trail with John Bozeman himself. For the next four years he drove freight wagons from Fort Benton to the Montana mining camps. In 1868 he homesteaded with his two brothers in the Chesnut Valley south of Cascade. In those days there was public grazing and as long as a rancher had control of water there was little reason to actually own land. When the advent of the Northern Pacific Railroad in the 1880s helped bring about the end of public grazing the idea of private property ownership became more appealing. And through a tough combination of luck, savvy, and a willingness to "gamble," Henry Sieben acquired and disposed of land until finally the Sieben Ranch north of Helena and the Adel Ranch south of Cascade became permanent parts of his legacy. The wheel tracks of the Mullan road are still visible through portions of the Sieben ranch. It is said that during his freighting days Henry came across the Mullan road and said, "someday I'm going to own this place."

"I guess there's a real parallel between our great-grandfather's gambling spirit and the risks we're taking with the cattle we've just trailed over the Divide," Chase mused. "Instead of raising these cattle from calves, we bought them in hopes that cattle prices will make it pay off this fall."

"This is good grass," Scott explained, "and we expect that these 560-pound-average steers will weigh around 825 pounds by the end of the grazing season in late September." At that time the cattle will be sold to an order buyer, loaded up at the Avon shipping docks, and transported to feedlots where an average weight of about 1,150 pounds will be attained by January.

For at least 30 years the Hibbard family has been driving cattle from Tenmile Creek near Helena, over Priest Pass, and onto the summer pastures of their Dog Creek holdings. "We really don't envision much change in our basic operation here," said Scott. Indeed, it was easy to see why. Despite the dry 1985 spring the land and grass appeared to be in excellent condition — the result of generations of wise land stewardship by the Hibbards.

In order to prevent overgrazing of their west-slope Continental Divide rangeland, the Hibbards have set up a rotation system whereby the grassy parks and forestlands east of Dog Creek are used during the early to mid-summer period only every other year. In 1986, for example, the cattle would be driven to the west of Dog Creek about the first of June to begin their assigned duty of gaining 300 pounds or so during the summer. By mid- to late July the cattle are driven across Dog Creek, to graze on about four sections of mostly deeded land on each side of the creek.

Outside of an occasional maverick human, there are no problems with predators. However, it is not unusual for a few cattle to be missing at the end of the grazing season — perhaps a close encounter with a train below Blossburg, or maybe the earlier-than-anticipated contents of someone's freezer. However, the response was quick to the question of why Sieben does not run sheep here. "Too many coyotes!" Scott exclaimed. Besides, according to Chase, "the timber's too thick to be able to control sheep."

For management purposes the 100 or so cows and calves are kept separate from the steers in different, smaller pastures. The steers range much better than cows, often ending up in rough country while the "cows won't go a step farther than they have to to find good grass."

As ranchers working both sides of the Great Divide, the Hibbards are in a good position to make comparisons. It's noticeably colder on the west side with a shorter growing season that starts later and ends earlier, Scott explained. The higher precipitation on the west side really shows up in the composition of grasses, stands of which are much thicker, Chase observed. This is partly because west slope soils are more mineral-rich, he said.

As a new column of dark rain clouds began to build and head toward the Divide, Scott remarked on how often he had been caught in storms in Dog Creek that "just didn't make it over the Divide."

The center of the Hibbards' Dog Creek holdings is occupied by a big red barn that was owned by one Dominic Bruno — a moonshiner who fronted as a dairy farmer. It seems that Bruno had cooperators in moonshiners' cabins all over the surrounding hills and forests. Every week or two he would run a pack string loaded with grain to supply the moonshiners with their necessary raw materials. At about the same frequency he would travel to Butte to deliver his multiple products: dairy cans with milk on top with a convenient false bottom to separate the whiskey below. A man had to be enterprising to make it along the Continental Divide in those days.

The Hibbards appreciate as much as anyone the problems confronting agriculture today. Although attracted to ranching as a lifestyle, they stress that that alone will not insure economic survival. Chase sees increasingly tough times in the cattle business as changes in dietary preferences and other factors will make the going even more difficult. The survivors in the cattle industry are going to have to be "more efficient in figuring out ways of cutting costs and increasing production," Chase predicted. "In short, the operation has to be run as a business. There will be no panacea in the marketplace."

The popular romantic images of western ranching can fade quickly when one becomes aware of the incredibly hard work involved. The cattle drivers had been up since five o'clock that morning and were only now able to take a brief break before riding back over the Divide to the Lazy B in search of stray steers. And this had been an easy day. Unloading cattle at midnight, feeding them in 30-below-zero weather, tending sick livestock are all in the line of what often turns out to be a 16-hour day.

"Why do I do it? I'll tell you when I find the answer," Scott said. Later, at a more thoughtful moment, Scott and Chase reflected on the rewards of being one's own boss, working outside, and being part of the land itself. Finally, both men agreed that a lot of the reason for the hard work with no guaranteed monetary return is because this is part of their heritage. Their roots go deep in this place, with these meadows, these forests, these wandering cattle, these feelings for the land on both sides of the Great Divide.

Neither Chase or Scott gives much thought to the fact that their ranch straddles the Divide. Both are far too occupied in the day-to-day management of surviving in the cattle business to dwell on what it means to drive a herd of cattle from the headwaters of one ocean to those of another.

Helena-area rancher Chase Hibbard (left) rides his Continental Divide cattle range west of Priest Pass.
Having just crested Priest Pass, the herd of 500 steers drops down the western slopes of the Divide toward Dog Creek. BILL CUNNINGHAM
PHOTOS

A Cattle Drive over Priest Pass

"I expect that we'll be on top of Priest Pass with our 500 steers by around 9:00 a.m.," said Scott Hibbard, manager of the Lazy B ranch, part of the expansive Sieben Live Stock Company headquartered out of Helena. I was arranging to meet the June 5 cattle drive over the Continental Divide with camera in hand as the wandering herd, dogs and a dozen horseback riders ascended from the headwaters of the Atlantic Ocean to greet the nation's backbone.

The day began in Helena with a typical early June rain shower, but by the time I reached Priest Pass 15 miles west of Helena, coming from Dog Creek on the western slopes, dramatic sunshine was filtering through high clouds. Perfect for pictures, I thought, as I hiked up and down the Divide ridge north of the Pass waiting for the ascending herd and herders. Time passed and the weather changed, as it often does along the Divide, with a stiff west wind accompanied by intermittent driving rain. Yes, my picture sunlight had vanished along with the upcoming herd. Or at least, so it seemed. Finally by 10 a.m. three black yearling steers charged over the Divide followed by a lone horseman. Is this all there is to it?

A fleeting conversation with the rider, Whit Hibbard, revealed that the main herd would be along shortly but that this had been the "toughest drive ever" over the Divide, with lots of cattle straying off into the heavy timber. Soon, hundreds of steers heading to summer pasture on the west side of the Divide, being driven by a dozen riders, emerged into the open grassy park that makes up historic Priest Pass.

"This is the part of ranching that I really enjoy, getting out on the ground," said Chase Hibbard of the Sieben Live Stock Company, "but it seems that I spend at least sixty to seventy percent of my time in the office." After the steers were trailed down the west side of the Divide for about 1½ miles to a holding pasture we had time for a visit. The first order of the day, however, was to compare the beginning head count of 6 a.m. that morning, 501 steers, to the 474 that the herders had on hand at the moment. "Not good," Scott said. "We've got 27 steers running loose in the timber, but we'll pick them up between now and tomorrow morning when we bring the cows and calves over." Such is the life of a cattleman. Scott reported a month later that all but four were accounted for and he knew where those were.

Outfitting Along the Divide

It's hard to compare flatland farming in Iowa to outfitting along the rugged Continental Divide in the heart of the Bob Marshall Wilderness. But Ann and Max Barker, owners of the JJJ Guest Ranch west of Augusta, are in a position to do so. They've done both.

The Barkers, now in their 50s, have worked with stock and on the land most of their lives, so perhaps their transition to dude ranching and horse outfitting in Montana wasn't as big a jump as it sounds. Max's first exposure to Montana was as a forester with Northern Pacific in the Swan Valley more than 20 years ago. He later returned to Iowa to run a large farm but "once you're exposed to the Rockies you can't get it out of your blood," he admitted.

In 1975 the Barkers leased the farm and spent the summer in Montana looking for a foothills cattle ranch. They wanted a place with lots of green grass, having seen enough of the dry prairie country. It didn't take long for them to realize that the multi-million dollar price tag of such an operation made it nothing more than a pipedream.

The following winter Ann urged her husband to go back to Montana in search of a foothold in the country. "It was one of Ann's better ideas," says Max. The search for a place ended up around Augusta after a fellow in the Forest Service had described it to Max as "real horse country." Max just happened to stumble onto a for-sale sign at a place up the Sun River Canyon in Mortimer Gulch called the JJJ.

Before long the Barkers had made a deal and by that fall they were outfitting in the Bob Marshall Wilderness. At the time, the place "wasn't much to look at," Barker said. After putting up a new lodge, remodeling the cabins and running fencelines, the Barkers have transformed the JJJ from a run-down hunting lodge to a beautiful dude ranch in the heart of the spectacular Rocky Mountain Front just east of the Continental Divide.

The outfitting part of the business had to be built from the ground up, with only four hunters booked the first season. Four years later they had 60 hunters and two or three summer pack trips. Today, the Barkers are still among some 50 professional outfitters in the "Bob." Nearly a dozen of these outfits operate along the Rocky Mountain Front and along the Continental Divide.

Max and Ann enjoy the dude-ranching end of the operation more than the hunting. They house guests in their rustic lodge on the edge of a 2½-million-acre expanse of wilderness/roadless country and lead an annual average of six summer horseback trips of seven to 10 days with six to eight guests. But because of the lure of big game animals

Above: *The Chinese Wall in the Bob Marshall Wilderness. According to Augusta outfitter Max Barker, words cannot describe the feeling of being back on the Divide in the heart of Bob Marshall country.*
Right: *Max and Ann Barker's JJJ Guest Ranch west of Augusta originates numerous pack trips to and along the Continental Divide each year.* BILL CUNNINGHAM PHOTOS

such as elk, deer, moose, sheep, goats and even grizzlies on a very limited basis, the Barkers can book five hunters for every person booked on a summer pack trip.

When Max first came into the country, wilderness meant "expanses without fences, without roads and without people. To be able to get on a horse and ride all day long without running into a damn barbed wire fence was heaven." So to the Barkers, the Bob Marshall Wilderness was and is "a million acres of heaven."

There is a romantic illusion that outfitting in the Bob Marshall is a paid vacation. In fact it is mostly hard work, sometimes with marginal return on a huge investment in horses, feed, equipment and vehicles. On top of all this is a growing uncertainty about outfitting regulations and nonresident hunting licenses — the bread and butter of fall outfitting in the Bob. The Barkers and other professional outfitters stay with it because of the freedom it provides them and the gratification they get in helping others "completely relax and renew their spirits," as Barker put it.

Max Barker has worked hard to protect the wildlife-rich "de facto" wilderness of Deep Creek in the Rocky Mountain Front adjacent to the JJJ. "What I really want is to see the country stay as it is," he reflects, "but that just isn't going to happen without wilderness." Although there are many challenges facing the future of wilderness outfitting, Max states flatly that the worst thing that could happen to his business would be "oil and gas development with roads" next to the JJJ.

Barker believes strongly that wilderness should not only be preserved for posterity but also should be available for compatible recreation, such as outfitting. "The jury's still out," he said with respect to a new wilderness management process called "Limits of Acceptable Change," which the Forest Service is beginning to test in the Bob Marshall Wilderness complex. Barker worries that managers believe they can deal with "perceived problems of overuse" in the wilderness "with an electronic computer without hiring any more experienced people on the ground."

Barker figures that he crosses the rugged Continental Divide with a pack string over such Bob Marshall passes as Teton and Spotted Bear at least 15 times a season. Once, while riding a steep cliff trail over the north end of the Chinese Wall one of their guests, a woman from Virginia, became so "terrified" that she couldn't go forward or backward. "At times like that you just have to fall in love with your horse," laughed Ann, "and by golly she made it."

The idea of the Continental Divide has always intrigued Barker, even before he and Ann began outfitting in the country. "I'm thrilled to death to be back on the Divide. There are just no words to describe it."

Tending her flock. Sheepherder Michelle O'leary rides the high Continental Divide meadows of upper Odell Creek in the heart of southwest Montana's Centennial Mountains. One of three herders working for the U.S. Sheep Experiment Station, Michelle sees to it that her band of 2,140 ewes and lambs are continually moved to areas of good feed so that her wooly wards gain maximum weight with minimum impact on the land. When the author visited with Michelle on an August day, she already had been herding along that remote stretch of the Divide for more than a month, and would remain there until early September. Indeed, she seemed to be thriving on the solitude. Some losses to predators are inevitable, but as of that mid-season date only one sheep had been lost to a black bear—testimonial to Michelle's ability to keep track of her flock. After her visitor confessed to long-term romantic illusions of being a sheepherder, Michelle exclaimed, "you should be here when you're wet, with a wet sleeping bag and tent day after day!" BILL CUNNINGHAM

Above: *A climber finds the Continental Divide to be the easiest route down Eighteenmile Peak, which looms in the background.* BILL CUNNINGHAM

Top left: *Here the Divide twists and turns across the vast treeless landscape of the Italian Peaks.* RICK GRAETZ

Bottom left: *From the top of Eighteenmile Peak the Divide is difficult to identify as it weaves southeast across plateaus and mountains toward the Lima Peaks.* BILL CUNNINGHAM

18-Mile Peak Winter Expedition

The thought was somehow irresistible. And soon it sank in so as to consume every waking moment as well as some non-waking moments during the week before the trip. Our goal was simple and straightforward: to climb the highest point on Montana's portion of the Continental Divide — 11,141' Eighteenmile Peak, the highest point of the Great Divide between Banff to the north and the Wind River Range of Wyoming to the south — a distance of more than 1,000 miles.

An additional element made our goal even more enticing. We would attempt a winter ascent. We had visions of being the first to do so and, as far as we know, we were! Our pre-trip planning revealed that a summer climb of Eighteenmile is a walk-up, but we really had no idea how conditions would be in the winter. There was only one way to find out.

Rick Graetz, Rick Reese and I had long regarded the remote southwestern location of the peak as Montana's hidden corner. Indeed, it was hard to find people who were even aware of, let alone personally familiar with, this southernmost extension of Montana's Divide country.

Eighteenmile Peak reaches skyward in a narrow extension of the proposed 52,000-acre Italian Peaks Wilderness in the Beaverhead National Forest. Although the peak and its immediate environs are as wild, beautiful and distinct as any of Montana's diverse wildlands, it is not part of the small 12,900-acre Italian Peaks "consensus" Wilderness — a conflict-free boundary readily agreed to by almost everyone.

The three of us left Helena the morning of February 22, wondering how close to the mountain we could get by car. Knowing that the Big Sheep Creek road wound some 25 miles from I-15 to the vicinity of Eighteenmile Peak, we had visions of slogging along 20 miles of unplowed road with heavy packs. As it turned out, our car ground to a halt in unplowed snow a scant five miles from where we would establish our base camp at the foot of the mountain.

By that evening we were leveling snow for our tent and searching for a clear view of our lofty destination. We were not to be rewarded. The entire stretch of the Divide was obscured by low clouds. We crawled into our sleeping bags that night wondering if we would even see the peak the next day during our ascent.

At 6:30 the following morning we arose to a brilliant view of the peak. The air was clear and cold — two degrees below zero, undoubtedly normal for late February at 8,400', but still it took a while for the vital juices to flow. With the rising sun at our backs the skyline of the Great Divide stood out with crystal clarity. The high winds of yesterday had calmed to a breeze — still bone-chilling at subzero temperatures.

We set out toward the headwaters of Bear Creek with ropes on our skis, slogging through the worst possible conditions — a hard thin crust atop three feet of seemingly bottomless sugar snow. By 10 a.m. we reached the foot of the northeast summit ridge — our most likely route. The incessant, high winds that were beginning to pick up had blown most of the open ridge free of snow leaving, in places, a thin, hard layer of ice.

The peak glistened in the midmorning light looking so near and yet being so far. Exhilarated by a feeling of certain success we began our steep climb. It was a process of alternatingly walking on bare ground, breaking through several feet of snow, gingerly balancing on icy rocks and cautiously stair-stepping up the long, 70 percent slope of hard-packed ice. Lacking crampons and ice axes we had no choice but to forge steadily upward using our ski poles while erasing from our minds the thought of sliding off into the rocks below. We accomplished this erasure by not looking down as we climbed.

As last we were there! At 11:30 a.m. on February 23, 1985, we stood atop the highest point on Montana's Continental Divide, feeling as though we could see all of the Northern Rockies. The brilliant light and limitless clear air allowed us to see for many miles along the Divide — from the Grand Tetons to the southeast to the Gravellies, Lima Peaks and Centennials. To the north we saw the Pioneers, and to the west the Lemhi and Lost River Ranges of Idaho. But most impressive was the Great Divide itself. We found ourselves captivated by the stunning view of the 2,000' sheer escarpment of the north face of 10,998' Italian Peak — a Continental Divide wilderness mountain that forms the southernmost tip of Montana.

Our magnificent two-mile walk southeast along the Divide was made even more exhilarating by a constant wind gusting occasionally to 50 miles per hour. When we arrived on line, with a low pass a mile to the west on the Idaho side of the Divide, we intercepted the ferocity of a natural wind tunnel that made walking upright an almost impossible task. Wind, wild beauty, snow sculpture and vast, unspoiled panoramas combined to

Double Divide Bike Ride. *With one of the major climbs accomplished, bicycle riders top MacDonald Pass 15 miles west of Helena. The Double Divide Ride (DDR) is an annual 141-mile bike tour sponsored each September by the Helena Bicycle Club. In 1985, 40 serious bicyclists participated in the event, including the author's 15-year-old son Bryn. The cyclists leave Helena, climb over MacDonald Pass and spend the night in Lincoln west of the Divide. On the second day the intrepid riders climb Flesher Pass en route back to Helena. DDR Director Eric Grove describes the tour as the "most scenic and realistic bike loop out of Helena." The ride offers ample challenge and exhilaration, as the pedal pushers top the Continental Divide twice in as many days for a vertical climb of more than 4,000 feet. Since its 1980 inception, DDR has had a history of marginal weather. In 1985 the ride had to be postponed a week when the Divide was cloaked in a foot of fresh snow on the slated weekend of September 7-8. CAROLYN CUNNINGHAM*

make our trek along the Great Divide of Montana's hidden corner an unforgettable experience.

As we descended a steep tree-covered ridge into our base camp at the head of the Bear Creek basin I was again struck by the significance of the Continental Divide as the watershed of our nation and the source of great rivers and wilderness solitude.

As it turned out we had been given a fleeting "window of opportunity." The next day brought foul weather. The entire Divide was enveloped in a high storm system that hid all but the lower slopes. The view from our climb was a special gift from the wild country high atop Montana's Continental Divide.

A classic post-and-pole "worm" fence cuts across the spacious Big Hole Valley toward the distant snow-capped peaks of the southern Bitterroot Range. GEORGE WUERTHNER

Ranching in the Big Hole

The wide-open country of the Big Hole Valley in southwestern Montana just east of the Continental Divide defies superlatives. As magnificent as the valley is, it is perhaps best known for the blue-ribbon trout stream that drains it. And the fact that the Continental Divide encloses the valley on three sides gives the Big Hole a feeling all its own.

I was visiting with Jack Hirschy, a third-generation Big Hole Valley rancher whose family owns a good part of the broad valley from "timberline to timberline" near Wisdom. Jack's grandchildren are the fifth generation growing up on one of the largest commercial cattle operations in western Montana. As we looked across the valley from the Hirschy home, Jack observed that the ranches in the Big Hole have something "in addition to cattle value; they have scenic value."

In about 1893 Jack Hirschy's grandfather filed for a homestead south of Wisdom next to his wife's cousin's place. The next year he brought his family to Dillon from Indiana on an "emigrant" train and then by wagon to the homestead. He also brought milk cows because cheesemaking was in his Swiss blood. After a couple of years they realized that the valley is just too high for anything but hay and beef production. Indeed, it takes a special breed to live year-round in the Big Hole. Jack aptly describes the winters as generally severe with six to seven months of continuous snow cover in the valley being common. The average of only *eight* consecutive frost-free days per year makes growing anything but hay a marginal proposition at best.

Over a period of generations the modest Hirschy homestead of 160 acres in 1893 has been built into a magnificent cattle ranch in one of the most beautiful intermountain valleys in the west. The extensive herd of cows, mostly angus, begins calving early in March with a good survival rate of about 90 percent. The cows are wintered at a lower-elevation ranch near Whitehall where they can forage along the Jefferson River. Meanwhile, the yearlings are fattening on hay in the Big Hole. By the end of May the cows are trucked back to the Big Hole and turned out onto the range.

The Hirschy grazing allotment on the adjacent Beaverhead National Forest extends to the Divide up to and south of 7,236' Big Hole Pass. Some of this higher grazing country near the Divide is deeded land in Isaac Meadows and along Pioneer and Ruby Creeks. The cows are normally turned onto the forest allotment by mid-June and taken off by the first of October.

Yearlings are kept off the high Continental Divide ranges because of their wide-ranging tendencies. However, the cows and calves are at home there and can be more easily managed. Even so, a hired man lives at the nearby "1120 ranch" and rides the range on horseback almost every day. During the summer grazing season the cows and calves will gain about 200 pounds on the nutritious native grasses.

After reflecting on the relationship between his place and the Great Divide, Jack described the Continental Divide as "the lifeline of the Big Hole. It's where our water, timber and recreation come from. At 6,400 feet elevation, our place goes almost up to the Divide. I wouldn't live anywhere else." Indeed, this love for the land shows on the land itself. The good condition of the range during the unusually dry spring of 1985 testified to the Hirschy family's refusal to overgraze. "We're not here today and gone tomorrow," said Jack, "we've been here for close to 100 years and we want to be around for at least another 100."

Looking at the miles of classic old post-and-pole, zig-zag "worm" fences on the place and the crumbling homesteaders' cabins scattered around the valley evoked images of the colorful history of the area. When Bannack played out, some of the miners drifted north and found placer gold in Pioneer Creek. The mining camp of Pioneer they founded is occupied now only by the ghosts of its past. The Hirschy ranch, which includes the abandoned

Big Hole rancher Jack Hirschy stands on the original homestead founded by his grandfather in 1893—the modest origin of one of Montana's most expansive cattle ranches.

townsite of Pioneer, was on the stage-freight route that went from Red Rock through the Big Hole Valley and over the Divide at Big Hole Pass to the riproaring mining town of Gibbonsville, Idaho.

Jack's father, Fred Hirschy, once met a fellow near the pass on Flyspeck Ridge driving a wagon loaded with pipe. The man's young son was tied onto the pipe so he wouldn't slide off going down the steep trail to Gibbonsville. When Jack was a young man he and his family often motored up the fairly gentle Montana side of the Divide in a Model T Ford. In order to descend the steep Idaho side of the Divide, trees were cut and tied to the back and dragged for extra braking. Up until the early '40s Jack helped trail cattle bought in the Salmon River country over the Divide.

Around the turn of the century a Dr. Wentworth died while traveling during the winter along North Sheep Creek about eight miles east of the Divide. His wife kept his frozen body for several months until the ground thawed out and then she buried him on the spot, just below the 1120 ranch.

Nowadays, a changing cattle market is resulting from overproduction of beef and growing health-consciousness of society. Hirschy believes that the market might be improved if grass-fed cattle are marketed directly to the consumer. Despite problems with the market, the Hirschy family is optimistic about the future — clearly attracted to the way of life of ranching in the Big Hole. The Hirschys are one of the few old Big Hole families still working the original family ranch for the production of red meat.

Top: *For more than 90 years Big Hole pioneer Leo Hagel has logged, mined, trapped and ranched in Montana's Continental Divide country.*
Bottom: *Animal hides strung across the road just east of Big Hole Pass work well as a "cattle guard."* BILL CUNNINGHAM PHOTOS

The Great Continental Divide Expedition

edited by Mark Meloy
— as Described by Members Mark
Meloy, Sanna Porte, Tracy Barrett
and Dan Dalphonse

Dan and Mark came up with the idea, one of the many eccentric notions one is apt to conjure during the abysmal stretch of cold gray days that follow Christmas in Montana. To hike the entire summer along the Continental Divide from our doorsteps in Helena to the Canadian border was a proposition that also captured the imagination of cohorts Sanna Porte and Tracy Barrett. The four of us would hike 600 miles of the wilderness heart of Montana.

By the end of May, all of us had tied up the loose ends of our lives and were each gainfully unemployed and free to pursue the many preparations necessary for an expedition of magnitude. We collected the necessary topographic maps and charted a route. Next we filled plastic containers with eight weeks worth of backpacking food and found participants among our families and friends willing to deliver the food supplies to designated trailheads of highway crossings at weekly intervals along our route.

Despite the fact that none of us had much experience in the finer points of long distance backpacking, our elaborate preparations resulted in a nearly trouble-free 60-day hike. Since our supplies were delivered to us, we would not have to emerge from the wilderness until the end of the hike at Waterton Lakes, Canada.

As the crow flies, we looked at a straight line of 200 miles from Helena to Canada. Our actual route zigzagged that line and tripled the distance so that we might see the entire breadth of the wilderness literally lying north of our doorstep: the Scapegoat, Bob Marshall and Great Bear Wildernesses and Glacier National Park.

After a champagne brunch on the Fourth of July, we ascended the first hill above Helena and headed for the ridgeline of the Continental Divide and two straight months of hiking bliss and blisters.

The following passages offer personal impressions of our trek into the great wilderness of the Continental Divide. They are drawn from our four separate journals.

July 4th — We began the trip at the end of Rodney Street in Helena. Four of us would hike 600 miles with 50 pounds in each pack. Passing through four great wildernesses, we

Sanna Porte

Tracy Barrett

Dan Dalphonse

Mark Meloy
MARK MELOY PHOTOS

would cross only five paved highways before reaching our destination in Canada. We were to be a tribe of wilderness nomads for nine weeks, though I suspect that any measurement of time would be inadequate to describe the length of this journey. The second we left Rodney Street, our hearts bounded with joy. We freed ourselves into the wilderness, into new lives, into what seemed like a different time.

July 11th — We found few maintained trails in the drainages of Ten Mile Creek, Canyon Creek, the Little Blackfoot River and Nevada Creek, all emerging from that first long, dry stretch of the Divide. We bushwhacked through dense lodgepole forests, plowed through the high grasses of open meadows, climbed talus slopes of huge granite boulders and sometimes were able to follow wagon roads left by miners nearly a century ago. The abundance of wildlife was obvious from the pervasive large animal droppings and tracks indicating the presence of elk, moose, deer, bear, lynx, bobcat and cougar. Perhaps this country will someday be protected as wilderness; much of it is undeniably wild.

July 12th — We saw no more than a trickle of water the first week on the Divide. Each evening one of us would drop a mile or two down a dry creek bed until a rock basin or grass-covered hole could be found, potholes of water to fill our plastic bottles.

July 15th — It took us 10 days to reach the paved road at Rogers Pass, beyond which were the beginnings of the "official" wilderness journey in the Scapegoat Wilderness Area. Having spent that time without adequate water for washing, our grubby spirits soared when we reached Heart Lake.

It's great being around so much water; we can drink all the teas we want and use water without a second thought. It's raining; Sanna plays "Greensleeves" on the trail-battered guitar.

July 16th — Our diet is mostly dried beans and rice cooked in a lightweight pressure cooker. Cutthroat trout provide a

The Chinese Wall. MARK MELOY

July 24th — On the South Fork of the Flathead River, where Gordon Creek enters, we camped on a sandbar covered with huge cottonwood trees. The river brings to the dense evergreen forests welcome spatterings of deciduous green, willows and cottonwood. Sand ants are abundant. They crawl through our gear in search of morsels amongst our dry, well-packaged food.

July 30th — Having begun our second traverse of "the Bob," we found ourselves in high gear on a "mainline" trail above Big Salmon Lake. The heavily used campgrounds are a mess. Particularly, the smell of uric acid from horses drives us away from the regular camping spots. We bushwhacked our way over to a small gravel bar on Big Salmon Creek, laid out our camp and whomped up a batch of freeze-dried Romanoff — so named for its notoriety in causing one to go roamin' off with a roll of toilet paper.

August 8th — We got our first glimpse of the fabled Chinese Wall after a long climb up through White River Pass. We followed the trail along the base of that magnificent limestone wall until we found our split-level home for the night among the monolithic boulders, the beargrass and the gnarled pines. Enchanted country.

Tracy and I put together the feast — garbanzo beans and huckleberry bannock bread — while Dan and Mark climbed a steep chute to the top of the wall. We heard their triumphant yodeling and saw them wave up there in the sunset. I expected them to return with the Ten Commandments.

August 11th — Today we climbed the divide separating the White River from the South Fork of the Flathead. It occurred to me that the names of the surrounding mountains were peculiar yet nonetheless accurate. Alongside the Chinese Wall were Sphinx Peak, Amphitheater Mountain and the Pagoda.

August 15th — This morning we dragged our post-cache-delivery-day hangovers up the Spotted Bear River and set a record for the least miles travelled in one day. The cure was foil-baked, butter-basted trout, sprinkled with dill weed and whatever else happened out of our spice bag.

August 17th — Near the bottom of Switchback Pass we met a fellow who, having come south from Glacier Park, claimed we wouldn't run into many tourists there because the grizzlies had devoured most of them. Of course we didn't buy it, but the sweat on his brow and his fast, nervous pace made us more cautious as we dropped into the Great Bear Wilderness.

tasty supplement to this meager fare. Spent the morning at Webb Lake frying bannock bread and trying to scrub the grime out of our clothes. Then we lit out for North Fork Falls, following the West Fork of the Blackfoot River from its headwaters. We see it shimmering down below us, or eye-to-eye as we cross portions of it. We camped by it tonight. What a delight to have the river making lullabies right at our feet.

The first thirsty two weeks of this trip have taught me to cherish pure water above all things. I lay myself down in the icy North Fork of the Blackfoot tonight and completely covered my scalded, torn and bitten body with the water's sacred balm. I held on to the boulders and let the current massage my knotted muscles and took great gulps of it. I don't care if I ever drink anything else again.

July 20th — The trail took us to a small, open saddle which was our trail over the Divide. The view from the ridge was stupendous; Scapegoat Mountain must be 15 miles of jagged 300 foot cliffs dotted with limestone caves and peaked by 9,000-foot crests. We cut across the talus slopes below the cliffs and glided on automatic pilot to the end of an "endless" 15-mile day. Halfmoon Park was our destination, named for a crescent of cliff walling in the west side of a huge fire-born meadow.

July 22th — In four days we would hike the width of the Bob Marshall Wilderness Area. My pack is letting me know what heavy really means. I suppose I have to get as hard as the country I'm walking through. Today a tree stopped me cold in the trail; straight and tall, it told me it was as alive as I.

August 19th — Dean Lake re-christened itself last night with the perfect reflections of the constellations on its black velvet surface. We've had no qualms about renaming everything —mountains, lakes, creeks — whose names don't suit our fancy. Besides, Dean has thrown his name around enough up here. This one is ours. Lake Cassiopeia gave us an icy morning swim, our shouts of ecstasy echoing off the peaks above.

After an award winning breakfast of bannock French toast with huckleberry syrup, we wended our way down the flowery and rocky meadows, stopping to look at mountain goats and spiders. We lost about two hours in fascination at the activities of the millions of spiders who were spinning their final webs of summer. They seem intent upon lacing up the entire woods with their sparkling strands before they die.

August 20th — We tromped from wilderness right into Vacationland USA: Schaefer Airfield. What a rude shock. Million dollar dudes gallumphing smartly by on horseback — superhighway trails.

Our escape was down river. We crossed a howling trackless wasteland where the 1964 flood had created 50 years of gravel pit on either side of the river. We had just decided to go down to the water when the trail perversely took its own rein and went uphill. For miles. Straight up. The kind of situation that makes me kick the trail and swear and moan. No one can tell me that it isn't the trail's fault that it was built the way it was. Hocky puck. That trail knows exactly what it's doing, and it's plain sadistic. You can hear it sneer and snicker at your grief, that kind of trail.

August 21 — The climb up Devil's Hump turned out to be another thigh burner. Our rewards were a view at the top and huckleberry heaven. We picked more than two gallons of the thickest, hugest, juiciest hucks ever. We are raving maniacs about these berries. We need clinical help — a Huckleholics Anonymous. Just when we have promised ourselves to go straight, the huckles reach out and drag us kicking and screaming into the bushes. There's no hope.

August 22 — The censors deleted most of my journal entry today. Ever try to divvy up crackers in a drenching down pour? We arrived at Marias Pass wet, clamoring for dry. My brother greeted us with our 7th cache of food, offered little more than a few words of encouragement and sped off in his fancy sports car, the latest rock and roll music blaring through its plastic windows. I felt ready to surrender to the nearest Holiday Inn. Instead we retreated to the cold, soaking wet tents and comforted ourselves with memories of sunny yesterdays.

August 24 — On the hike from East Glacier to Two Medicine Lake, the trail was lined with dead, windblown

Top: *Devil Creek*
Bottom: *Kevan Mountain*.
MARK MELOY PHOTOS

trees — weird, mysterious surroundings, where we met a band of Blackfeet Indian kids. All were from Browning and were taking part in a spiritual ritual. We stopped and talked a long time. Strange experience —we white intruders with our fancy, flashy, expensive equipment, getting back to nature in the company of these Blackfeet who consider this wild area home.

We watched them scamper like antelope to an overlooking ledge, to spread their arms to the sky and sing a prayer.

August 25th — Got up at the proverbial crack of dawn and lit out for Old Man Lake. Windy day. Half seriously, we were advised by two rangers at the trailhead to take our snow shovels. We laughed at them and set out, the wind gathering its furor as the cold front set in from Canada. It was a heady kind of violence, exciting, sensuous. We felt as though Glacier Park were saying, "Alright, pilgrims, you've had a jolly time lollygagging up to this point. Now you're in the big time, and I'm going to show you who is in charge here." Our jovial spirits were daunted by the pressing wind and rain. We arrived at Old Man Lake on the verge of hypothermia, the wind gusting to nearly 60 miles per hour on Dan's wind gauge.

I think this a beautiful place but I can't stop shivering long enough to hold my vision steady so I can see it. We're weathering a damn hurricane!

August 27th — Tracy no longer asks for a crisp salad, she prays for dry boots. Her boots would surely rot if it were warmer. At Sperry Glacier, we put our tent in a designated spot of the campground, a somewhat sheltered spot between two rock walls. That night we learned a lesson as old as the Boy Scout manual. Don't tent in a gully. It rained and snowed all night, and the deluge nearly washed us away. I still think we should sue those government goat tenders up there for putting the campground where they did. It will be difficult, however, for the jury to set damages sufficient to cover the pain of having slept in a creek. Ten or twenty thousand dollars ought to cover the cost of cruel and unusual muscle strain caused by packs twice as heavy with wet gear.

September 1st — It rained and snowed all the remaining days of our trip. Our spirits were low ... we were all in a stupor of cold and beauty of Glacier Park ... we drifted to the end of the trip.

September 2nd — After 12 solid days of rain, snow and wind in the alpine meadows of Glacier Park, we awoke one morning to a wet, icy mist blowing from the top of Mount Cleveland to the small circle of tents in the Waterton River campground. In the first light, I gather wood for a large fire.

On that day we left the wilderness and crossed the border into Canada. There was no fanfare, no hooprah, not even a customs agent. Just a quiet forest dulled by low-flying clouds. Two strange, tomblike, narrow, pointed monoliths marked the border.

It was finished. Now we could only hope not to adjust to culture shock ... as we embraced civilization once again. We spent two months losing our minds so we could come to our senses. Now we have left a lot of our senses in the wilderness. That's okay. We'll be back.

Tour of the Proposed Continental Divide National Scenic Trail in Montana

Northern Region Forest Service Information Officer Jud Moore is a model of patience and accommodation. But even Jud's patience must have been strained as he tried to explain to the would-be Continental Divide traveler on the other end of the line that his plan for a motorcycle ride along the crest of Montana's Continental Divide wasn't really feasible. It took some doing to convince the man that the combination of rugged terrain and wilderness protection along much of the Divide meant that he would need to find another mode of transportation, preferably foot or horseback. "I sure hope that you can clarify what the CDNST is all about," Jud said pleadingly.

The National Trails System Act of 1968 (P.L. 90-543) mandated a study of the proposed Continental Divide National Scenic Trail (CDNST), a study completed by the now-abolished Bureau of Outdoor Recreation in 1977. Of all the long-distance national trails, the proposed 3,100-mile trail along or near the spine of the continental United States from Canada to Mexico is the most magnificent. The study recommended creating the trail and in 1978 Congress formally established the CDNST. The same legislation ordered the preparation of a Comprehensive Plan for the management and use of the trail, but in the words of the privately-funded Continental Divide Trail Society, "The Forest Service continues to sit on the ... plan for the trail — now more than four years overdue! It's time to shake it loose."

A driving force behind the establishment and proper use of the CDNST is James R. Wolf, an avid backpacker, naturalist and conservationist. Jim was instrumental in forming the Society, which performs the vital function of making route recommendations, monitoring agency planning and management and fostering a national constituency for the trail. An excellent set of CDNST guides with detailed mile-by-mile recommended routes, can be obtained from the Society at Box 30002, Bethesda, Maryland 20814. The interim description of the proposed 805-mile-long route along Montana's portion of the Great Divide is contained in two volumes (Vol. 1: Northern Montana and Vol. 2: Southern Montana & Idaho) compiled by James R. Wolf. The books contain wildflower keys along with information on the history and wildlife of the Divide and are available at the above address.

A proposed route of the CDNST winds below the rugged crest of the Continental Divide in the high basins of the West Big Hole roadless area. BILL CUNNINGHAM

With more than 25 percent of the CDNST along Montana's Divide, the trail passes through incredibly diverse country — lofty mountain ranges, the varied habitats of different forest types and grasslands, and some of the most spectacular protected and un-protected wilderness lands in the lower 48. Although the trail has not yet been officially laid out, it already exists in fact. Old trails along much of the Divide are used by an ever-growing cadre of dedicated Continental Divide travelers. Before the final route of the CDNST is determined, we can expect that improvements will be made to enable trekkers to get away from roads and into more isolated back-country terrain.

Still, there are some conservationists who have valid concerns about the impact of trail usage on fragile alpine country and on threatened and endangered wildlife species, such as the free-roaming grizzly bear. Indeed, in its struggle for survival the grizzly doesn't need hordes of back-country recreationists invading its last secure habitat along the remote reaches of Montana's Great Divide wilderness country.

The reality is that these areas are becoming increasingly popular for wilderness-based recreation with or without

the Continental Divide National Scenic Trail. With sensitive management, proper routing and avoidance of publicity in key wildlife areas, the CDNST can be a positive influence on the protection of *de facto* wilderness lands along the Divide. Many such areas along Montana's Divide presently lack the formal protection of wilderness designation and should at least be managed to preserve the natural values and experiences sought by CDNST travelers.

A philosophy sometimes expressed by the Forest Service has been that the trail should expose the visitor to a variety of "cultural environments," such as logging clearcuts and mining operations. The Continental Divide Trail Society does not agree. The Society emphasizes the statutory direction to provide maximum outdoor recreation value and to provide for conservation and enjoyment of nationally significant scenic, historic, natural and cultural qualities — not exposure to human-dominated landscapes — as a guiding principle in routing the trail.

The general policy calls for the CDNST "to be located as close to the geographic Continental Divide as possible, but as far away as necessary to provide for safe travel and diverse recreation appeal, to be economically feasible and to keep environmental impacts to a minimum." Public lands and existing rights-of-way should be used as much as possible. In Montana, nearly all of the route described in the guide books is on public lands, compared to much lower percentages in more heavily-developed segments of the Divide to the south. Another important criterion is that the trail will meet the minimum standard for public safety based on anticipated use.

Trekking the CDNST

Each year one or more groups of hardy souls set out determined to hike the entire CDNST. Several years ago two members of the Rocky Mountain Women's Expedition became the first women to complete the trail from the Mexico border to Waterton, Canada. The women hiked an average of 15 miles per day on the 2,600-mile trip. After walking for six months and 24 days, one of the women, Lynn Wisehart, perhaps only half-jokingly said, "I hate hiking and I never want to carry a pack again. I'm into canoeing and mules — let them do the work."

About the same time two men in their 20s were near the beginning of a seven-month hiking trip over the same basic route, but from north to south. At Sula, Montana, as they took a break from carrying their 60-pound packs after a typical 15-mile day, one was asked if he was married. "Are you kidding?" he replied. "What woman would let her husband take a seven-month hike?"

PART III

Gateways
Along the Great Divide

There are literally thousands of identified topographical features along the approximately 800 miles of Montana's Continental Divide: mountain peaks, streams, basins, springs, ridges, lakes and those occasional gaps in the Divide we call passes. Of all these features, passes have stirred our interest and imagination the longest. Early-day Indian hunting parties, explorers, trappers and railroad surveyors were certainly not looking for mountains — for they were everywhere on the horizon — serving as barriers to whatever goal they had in mind. It was the legendary and sometimes illusive breaks in the mountains that they were seeking.

Of course the lowest gaps would be best for transportation corridors and Divide passes thus developed individual histories — some colorful, some momentous and some obscure. But because so much attention was, and is, focused on how best to cross the Continental Divide to whatever destination the history of the Great Divide in Montana is virtually synonymous with the history of its passes. There are countless gaps, saddles and cracks in the great barrier that divides the nation's watersheds. But there

are 54 passes along Montana's segment of the Divide that are significant enough to share a common distinction — each bears a name on the map. Following is a listing and brief description of each of these great gates of the great divide, in geographical order from north to south.

As an indication of the relative remoteness of the Continental Divide in Montana, 28 of the 54 named passes on the Divide remain roadless, traversed by only a foot or a horse trail. Virtually all of these pristine passes are in Glacier Park, the Bob Marshall Wilderness complex, or the Anaconda-Pintler Wilderness. Three of the passes are crossed by four-wheel-drive roads, nine by higher-standard gravel roads and the remaining 14 by paved highway ranging from four-lane Interstate to single-lane blacktop.

Elevations along the Divide in Montana vary by more than one vertical mile from 5,215' Marias Pass to 11,141' Eighteenmile Peak. Despite the constant up and down nature of the Divide itself, the elevations of its passes seem to follow a more uniform pattern. Only seven of the passes are between 5,000' and 6,000'; 22 dip to between 6,000' and 7,000'; 20 rise to between 7,000' and 8,000'; and four sit

between 8,000' and 9'000' —higher than most ridges and peaks of the actual Divide. Only one of these high passes — Cutaway — exceeds 9,000'.

1. Brown Pass (6,255') — Glacier National Park, Livingston Range. A trail and phone line top the pass linking Bowman Creek on the west and Olson Creek (east) below Thunderbird Glacier. It may have been named for Louis Brown, who married a Flathead woman.

2. Jefferson Pass (6,900') — Glacier Park, Livingston Range. This traverse joins Columbia-South Saskatchewan watersheds with Bowman Creek (west) and Valentine Creek (east). It is said to have been named for an early prospector and hunter of the region.

3. Kootenai Pass (5,700') — Glacier Park. This low pass links the Columbia-South Saskatchewan-Hudson Bay watersheds with Continental Creek and the Waterton River.

4. Ahern Pass (7,010') — Glacier Park. A dramatic trail winds up and over the Ahern Glacier from the Belly River to this cirque pass. Ahern and Mineral Creeks drain west to the Columbia with the Belly River being part of the Oldman-South Saskatchewan-Hudson Bay system. It was named for Lt. George Ahern, who crossed it during August 1890, with a unit of black soldiers from the 25th Infantry.

5. Swiftcurrent Pass (7,186') — Glacier Park. The trail to this pass takes off from the big curve in the Going-to-the-Sun Highway over the Divide to Many Glacier Chalet. It was once called Horse Thief Pass.

6. Logan Pass (6,649') — Glacier Park. On July 13, 1933, the Going-to-the-Sun Highway, crossing Logan Pass, was opened for traffic. The drive up McDonald Creek to the Garden Wall shelf with a steady 6 percent grade and down the east side to St. Mary Lake may well be the most spectacular in all the Rockies.

Profile of Elevation

This profile shows that, although Montana's Continental Divide features some stunning topography, it is local relief rather than elevation above sea level that makes it so. The overall uplift along the Divide in the U.S. tends to be higher in Colorado and even sunny New Mexico. However the extreme local relief on the Divide in Montana combined with its northern latitude create alpine and tundra conditions at lower elevations above sea level and make passes as forbidding as in higher mountains a thousand miles to the south.

U.S. Forest Service.

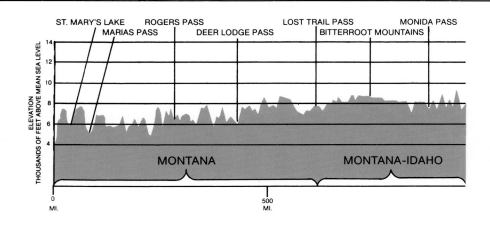

7. Gunsight Pass (6,946') — Glacier Park. This magnificent pass is reached by ascending St. Mary River from the Going-to-the-Sun Chalet. It was named in 1891 by George Bird Grinnell for its similarity to the rear sight of a rifle.

8. Red Eagle Pass (6,910') — Glacier Park. The trail heads up Red Eagle Creek to the glacier and pass, and down to the south along Nyack Creek to the Middle Fork Flathead River. In 1887 George Bird Grinnell named the pass for his friend Chief Red Eagle of the Blackfeet tribe.

9. Pitamakan Pass (7,510') — Glacier Park. From the east, the trail runs up Dry Fork past Cut Bank Pass and down Nyack Creek on the Columbia drainage side. It is the popular Cut Bank Pass of yesteryear's Indians. Abiel Tinkham of the Stevens Expedition mistakenly took it for Marias Pass when he crossed it in 1853 and it became known as False Marias Pass. It was named for the Blackfeet amazon, Pitamakan, who was known as the "Blackfeet Joan of Arc." Pitamakan wore male dress and led her warriors in raids in the Flathead country. Her real claim to fame was as a horse thief. As a girl, she proclaimed that she would wed any man who stole more horses on a given night than she could. No man ever did, so she remained unmarried until her death around 1850.

10. Cut Bank Pass (7,871') — Glacier Park. The trail climbs up the Dry Fork from Two Medicine Lake, with the north wall of the pass dropping vertically to Pitamakan Lake. The trail then runs south to Dawson Pass. Although steeper than Marias Pass, this pass provided a shorter route through the mountains and was thus preferred by the Blackfeet.

11. Dawson Pass (7,598') — Glacier Park. From Two Medicine Lake, the trail runs through Bighorn Basin to the pass and down Nyack Creek to the Middle Fork Flathead River. The pass was named for Thomas Dawson (Little

Dawson Pass in southern Glacier Park is accessible from the historic and, to the Blackfeet Tribe, the much revered Two Medicine area.
KENT KRONE

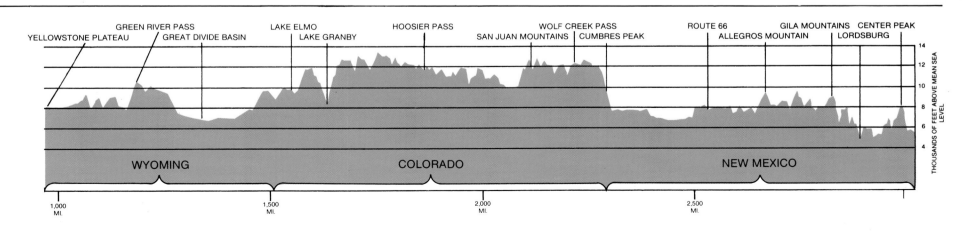

From the summit of the front range looking west, the Continental Divide forms the horizon across more than 20 miles of wilderness in the northern reaches of the Bob Marshall. BRUCE SELYEM

Montana Continental Divide Ranges With Peaks Above 10,000 Feet

Thirteen mountain ranges in Montana have peaks higher than 10,000 feet. Of these, four straddle portions of the Continental Divide.

Elev. Ranking	Range	Highest Peak
6	Bitterroot	Eighteenmile Peak (11,141')
8	Anaconda	West Goat Peak (10,793')
11	Lewis	Mt. Cleveland (10,466')
12	Highland Mtns.	Table Mtn. (10,223')

Highest Mountains on Montana's Continental Divide

Of the 100 highest summits in Montana, only three are located along the crest of the Continental Divide. All three are in the Italian Peaks portion of the southern Bitterroot Range.

Elev. Rank	Name	Elevation
73	Eighteenmile Peak (highest point on Montana's Continental Divide)	11,141'
79	Cottonwood Peak	11,024'
82	Italian Peak	10,998'

Although not on the list of Montana's 100 tallest peaks, the highest Montana point on the proposed route of the Continental Divide National Scenic Trail is 10,200' Elk Mountain, located about 10 miles southeast of Bannock Pass in southwest Montana.

Chief), son of American Fur Company trader Andrew Dawson.

12. Two Medicine Pass (7,675') — Glacier Park. An old Indian trail climbs Paradise Creek to the crest above Paradise Lake and the sublime country of the pass. The west descent is down Park Creek. Long ago, two groups of Blackfeet Indians showed up at the lake at the same time for their separate medicine lodge ceremonies. They held the rites together — thus the name.

13. Firebrand Pass (6,951') — Glacier Park. The trail runs west past Squaw Mountain and up Railroad Creek under Red Crow Mountain. Ole Creek drains off the pass to the west. Its name comes from firebrands that blew through the pass, causing extensive forest fires.

14. Marias Pass (5,215') — Just south of Glacier Park on U.S. 2. The highway runs up this gentle, wooded pass from the east along Summit Creek to the Theodore Roosevelt obelisk and John F. Stevens statue on top. Descent is along Bear Creek and the Middle Fork of the Flathead River. The Marias River was named in 1805 by Captain Lewis for the woman he hoped to marry, his cousin, Maria Wood. Maps as early as 1840 depicted the pass long before its official latter-day discovery in December 1889 by John F. Stevens. Construction of the Great Northern Railroad was then speeded up and completed in 1893. The false summit at the east foot of the pass was judged incorrectly to be the top in 1890 by engineers mapping the grade for the railway. Marias Pass is the lowest Continental Divide crossing not only in Montana, but also in the Rockies north of Mexico.

15. Muskrat Pass (5,974') — Southeast corner of the Great Bear Wilderness. From Marias Pass the Divide trends southeast for nearly 30 twisting miles before dropping to Muskrat Pass at the head of Muskrat Creek to the east and Cox Creek on the west side.

16. Badger Pass (6,278') — Just south of Muskrat Pass at the northeast corner of the Bob Marshall Wilderness. This beautiful wilderness pass is at the head of the North Fork, Birch Creek with Strawberry Creek draining to the west.

17. Gateway Pass (6,478') — Northeast portion of Bob Marshall Wilderness. From the west the trail climbs through the impressive Gateway Gorge to the high open plateau of Big River Meadows with the pass dropping abruptly off the edge of the Meadows to the South Fork, Birch Creek.

18. Teton Pass (7,775') — Northeast portion of Bob Marshall Wilderness just south of aptly-named Corrugate Ridge. From the east the trail climbs steeply along an open basin at the head of the West Fork, Teton River and down Bowl Creek to Gooseberry Park on the Middle Fork, Flathead River.

Continued on Page 90

Early Trips and Early Times over Big Hole Pass

In his 98th year, Leo Hagel of Gibbonsville, Idaho, is one of the last surviving early-day settlers of the Big Hole Pass stretch of Montana's Continental Divide. Possessed of a wiry frame and a keen mind, Hagel is able to recall details further back in time than the spans of most people's lifetimes.

Hagel first came to Salmon, Idaho, from Illinois in 1894 at the age of seven. In 1907 he made his first trip over Big Hole Pass into the Big Hole country. He and his brother were driving shorthorn cattle — "no Hereford cattle in those days, just good husky shorthorns." This was well before the present Big Hole Pass road was completed in 1910. In those days it took "four horses to pull a wagon" up the steep Flyspeck Ridge trail, which is a mile or so south of the present road.

Gibbonsville got all its supplies over Big Hole Pass. Hagel recalls when J.P. Lossel carried the mail over the Divide from Wisdom to Gibbonsville. It was earlier that Cloyd Wampler drove the first stage north from Bannack into the Big Hole to Wisdom and then over the Pass. Before a group of Big Hole Valley ranchers built the present Big Hole Pass road, stage passengers would have to get out and walk the final steep mile up Flyspeck Ridge to the Divide. During our visit, Hagel presented Jack Hirschy with the "walking plow" that was used to build the road over Big Hole Pass from 1907 to 1910.

Somewhere around 1913 Hagel homesteaded just east of the Divide in Isaac Meadows near the 1120 Ranch. By the time he got water and other improvements on the land, it took a full three years to prove up on the 160-acre homestead. He often welcomed Fred Hirschy overnight when the latter was trailing cattle over the Divide.

Although the settlement was long since abandoned, Leo remembers when people still lived and worked placer gold mining claims at Pioneer. The Wonderlake boys were the first in the area. They patented their claims before 1900 and were still working their quartz claims in 1913. Morgan Jones was caretaker for the Pioneer Gold Mining Company — a stock certificate of which was inherited by Jack Hirschy from his father. In exchange for his caretaking, Morgan got his board and any gold he found on the place. A pond nearby bears the name Morgan Lake.

Downstream from Pioneer is a bench containing the graves of two Pioneer citizens. One of those buried is a Mr. Benson who owned mining claims at Pioneer. During the

Top: *Big Hole rancher Jack Hirschy presents Leo Hagel with the original "walking plow" that was used to construct the Big Hole Pass road in 1907.* BILL CUNNINGHAM
Bottom: *Since the dirt road over Big Hole Pass was built 80 years ago, it has remained about the same.* BILL CUNNINGHAM

early 1900s two men passed through Pioneer and decided to camp next to another fellow's mining claim. The miner told them to move on but the travelers already had unloaded their packhorses and weren't about to leave. After an argument the miner grabbed his gun and killed one of the hapless would-be campers. The other got away. The body was thrown into a mine shaft where the bones remain to this day.

Leo Hagel worked at placer mining at Pioneer for nine years and believes that "there ought to be some pay in there

now." In 1919 he took $750 worth of Pioneer gold (996¼ pure out of a possible 1,000) to the San Francisco Mint. The going price was $20 an ounce in gold, and Hagel recalls, "the government paid its debts responsibly in those days."

During those early years Hagel also ran traplines at the head of Rock Creek, Moosehorn and other Big Hole River tributaries that flow from the Continental Divide. He trapped red fox, weasel, skunks, coyotes and "anything else we could get a dollar out of. We had to trap all winter long or else we'd starve." His favorite furbearer was the pine marten, which brought up to $15 — compared to about $5 for some other species. The best trapping for marten was on the Continental Divide itself.

"I've done damn near anything there ever was done to make a living, including cutting logs and piling slash for $1.50 per thousand board feet," Hagel said. He also used to cut cottonwood for 50 cents a cord plus board. For a while, he was cutting wild hay on the Pioneer and hauling it over the Divide to feed horses. "The Pioneer was the only place I knew where you could find native clover and timothy," which is pretty scarce nowadays, he explained.

Hagel remembers when snowshoe rabbits "were so thick along the Divide that they would pack the snow hard enough around trees to where you didn't even need snowshoes to walk on in the winter." Now, many kinds of birds, rabbits and other small mammals are mostly wiped out, a decline he attributes to the chemical spraying in the forest by a government that Hagel believes has grown far too big.

Toward the end of Prohibition, Montana was "wet" when Idaho remained "dry." Leo knew the location of five stills along the Continental Divide. A moonshiner by the name of Jack Lech bought legal liquor at Wisdom for about $4 a gallon, ran it over the Divide into Gibbonsville and sold his popular product for a profitable $20 a gallon. He often stayed with Hagel at the 1120 Ranch, insisting on rewarding his friend with a bottle of whiskey for his hospitality. Lech was crafty, never crossing the same place on the Divide twice in a row and he never was caught. However, one day he got into a violent argument with another moonshiner over his dog and was fatally shot.

Leo Hagel is among the last of a vanishing breed, a man who has spent more than 90 years along Montana's Great Divide mining, ranching, logging and trapping. He has witnessed incredible changes during his long, hard-working life along the Divide. He has seen what the land can produce in utilitarian terms, and through this he has developed strong feelings toward a country which he believes was "built by gold."

A September dusting of new snow at the head of the east-side Indian Creek basin enhances the view of remote White River Pass deep inside the Bob Marshall Wilderness. BILL CUNNINGHAM

An aerial view of Elk Park looking south displays Elk Park Pass, in the background, which drops steeply to the west into Butte. Interestingly, Elk Park itself is a high mountain basin—without a stream running through it. RICK GRAETZ

19. Sun River Pass (6,251') — northeast portion of the Bob Marshall Wilderness. This relatively easy pass is at the head of the wilderness waterway of the North Fork, Sun River. The west side descends Bowl Creek to Gooseberry Park.

20. Spotted Bear Pass (6,721') — eastern Bob Marshall Wilderness. An exposed, steeply-pitched wilderness trail heads up the heavily-timbered Rock Creek drainage and down the west side of the Divide to the Spotted Bear River.

21. Larch Hill Pass (7,702') — eastern Bob Marshall Wilderness. This magnificent gap in a high, subalpine larch forest defines the northern limit of the main Chinese Wall — a spectacular Continental Divide limestone escarpment rising 1,000' above the east-side basins for some 13 miles. To the west, the trail drops through an extensive area of the 1910 burn to the head of the remote White River.

22. White River Pass (7,626') — eastern Bob Marshall Wilderness. This remote gateway lies at the southern end of the Chinese Wall and is part of a major wilderness travel route across the Bob from the South Fork of the Sun River to the South Fork of the Flathead River on the west side.

23. Camp Creek Pass (7,200') — eastern Bob Marshall Wilderness. This opening in the Divide provides a scenic route from the Danaher east into Pearl Basin down to Indian Point on the West Fork of the South Fork, Sun River.

24. Observation Pass (7,444') — southeastern Bob Marshall Wilderness. This isolated pass provides a Divide crossing from the upper Danaher Basin east to the South Fork, Sun River.

25. Triple Divide (8,523') — southeastern Bob Marshall Wilderness. This point on the Divide is five miles south of Observation Pass at the headwaters of the South Fork of the North Fork, Blackfoot River, Rapid Creek of South Fork, Flathead River, and the Dry Fork of the North Fork, Blackfoot River. It is not to be confused with the true Triple Divide in southern Glacier Park which sends waters to three oceans.

26. Dearborn Pass (7,100') — northern portion of Scapegoat Wilderness. Here the trail runs up the wild Dearborn River to its extreme headwaters beneath 9,204' Scapegoat Mountain and to the west down the North Fork,

Blackfoot River drainage. It was named by Lewis and Clark for Henry Dearborn, Thomas Jefferson's Secretary of War.

27. Lewis and Clark Pass (6,323') — just north of Highway 200 and Rogers Pass. The pass is reached from the west by hiking a mile or so from the end of the Alice Creek road. This historic pass was crossed in 1806 by Captain Lewis and his men on their homeward journey. In 1853, Frederick W. Lander called it Lewis's Pass in one source and Railroad Pass in another.

28. Cadotte Pass (6,044') — This pass links the headwaters of Cadotte Creek to the east-side Middle Fork, Dearborn River. An ancient Indian traverse, called Blackfoot Pass, it was renamed for the French-Canadian guide, Pierre Cadotte, who was with Governor Isaac Stevens' Northern Pacific Railroad Survey of 1853. The pass was Stevens' original preferred route for the railroad.

29. Rogers Pass (5,609') — Northwest of Helena, this is the next crossing of the Divide by a road, Highway 200, south of Marias Pass some 145 miles to the north. Rogers Pass separates the Cadotte Creek/Blackfoot River drainage on the west side with the Middle Fork, Dearborn River to the east. The pass was named for the notable American engineer, Major A.B. Rogers, who surveyed it in 1887 while looking for a low Divide crossing for James J. Hill's Great Northern Railroad. Hill opted for Marias Pass, which is about 400 feet lower.

30. Flesher Pass (6,350') — Northwest of Helena, this pass accommodates paved state Highway 279 from Helena to Lincoln. Flesher was an early settler in the area.

31. Stemple Pass (6,349') — northwest of Helena and only about 11 Divide miles south of Flesher; the waters of Canyon Creek to the east and the North Fork, Poorman Creek to the west flow from this portion of the Divide. The pass, traversed by a good gravel road, was named for J.A. Stemple, who located the Stemple Mining District.

32. Mullan Pass (5,902') — west of Helena and traversed by both a good gravel road and the Northern Pacific Railway nearby, through a 3,850'-long tunnel at an altitude of 5,547'. The railroad passes by Austin, through the Mullan Pass tunnel and down the west side to the Dog Creek branch of the Little Blackfoot River. The pass was named for its discoverer, Lt. John Mullan (1853), who built the Mullan Military Road of some 624 miles from Walla Walla, Washington, to Fort Benton, Montana. The railroad was completed through the pass in 1882. In 1887, part of the Mullan tunnel caved in. During the period of repair, an army of wagons hauled passengers and freight over the top. Today, a rustic stone altar with log seats sits atop the Divide a mile or so north of the pass. It commemorates the first Masonic lodge meeting in Montana, held there during the summer of 1862 by Nathaniel P. Langford and three others. Langford later served as one of Yellowstone explorer Ferdinand V. Hayden's surveyors and went on to become the first superintendent of Yellowstone Park.

33. Priest Pass (5,994') — west of Helena, a good gravel road forks up Spring Creek rising steeply through heavy timber until reaching the open grasslands of the pass with a gentle west-side descent into Dog Creek. Valentine Priest, who was about to die of tuberculosis in the East, found a cure in the healthful climate of Montana. In the late 1870s he maintained the MacDonald Pass toll gate for Alexander MacDonald and concluded that he could build an easier toll-road crossing of the Great Divide. The result was his road over Priest Pass in 1879, which really was easier as well as being 300' lower. Priest Pass was the most popular crossing west of Helena until well into the age of the horseless carriage.

34. MacDonald Pass (6,323') — U.S. Highway 12 crosses this pass 15 miles west of Helena, connecting the Tenmile Creek drainage east of the Divide with the Little Blackfoot

Old mine buildings remind us of a colorful past at MacDonald Pass west of Helena. GARRY WUNDERWALD

River to the west. The original Tenmile toll road was built in 1870 by "Lige" Dunphy and managed until 1876 by Alexander MacDonald, who then became owner. MacDonald sold the road to David Gilmore in 1883. Three six-horse stages crossed the pass daily in the 1880s on the Helena-Deer Lodge run. The pass is the site of the renowned and rustic Frontiertown — a tourist attraction built by John Quigley. An excellent groomed cross-country ski trail system bypasses Frontiertown and winds for miles through heavy timber on the east side of the Divide.

35. Champion Pass (6,960') — north of Butte, this pass is crossed by a good gravel road that passes through extensive logging cuts up the Boulder River and down the west side along Peterson Creek to Deer Lodge. One can travel this portion of the Divide for several miles in either direction by means of dirt roads.

36. Elk Park Pass (6,374') — just north of Butte, this pass drops steeply to the west side from the high, open plateau of Elk Park. It is traversed by means of four-lane I-15 and a branch of the Burlington Northern Railroad.

37. Homestake Pass (6,356') — southeast of Butte, this pass is home to four-lane I-90 as well as the Burlington Northern Railroad, on their westward descents to the nearby Mining City. The pass got its name in the 1870s from a man named Spencer who made a modest mining stake between Miners Gulch and Niles Gulch.

38. Pipestone Pass (6,418') — southeast of Butte and only eight miles south of Homestake Pass, this gap contains Highway 10, which winds up Little Pipestone Creek to the forested top of the pass and down the steep hairpins of the east side along Blacktail Creek in the Jefferson River drainage. The Chicago, Milwaukee and St. Paul Railroad built its line under the pass through a 2,290' tunnel in 1909. At that time, the Northern Pacific controlled Montana's coal fields but the Montana Power Company had plentiful hydroelectric power. As a result, the Milwaukee Road was electrified all the way through the Rockies —a unique and successful experiment. The pass received its name from nearby Pipestone Hot Springs, where a ledge supplied pipe material to the Indians.

From the top of Homer Youngs Peak, the Big Hole Valley stretches northeast to a distant horizon formed by the Continental Divide in the Anaconda/Pintler Wilderness. BRUCE SELYEM

39. Deer Lodge Pass (5,902') — southwest of Butte, separating the Highland Mountains from the eastern Anaconda Range. The four-lane I-15 runs up the open grasslands of the upper Clark Fork over this nearly imperceptible pass and down the broad Divide Creek valley to the Big Hole River. The Utah & Northern feeder of the Union Pacific Railroad crossed this pass to Butte in 1881. The name is derived from tipi-shaped mounds of salt mineral formed by hot springs that attracted deer in the upper Deer Lodge Valley.

40. Cutaway Pass (9,036') — located along the northeastern crown of the rugged Anaconda-Pintler Wilderness, southwest of Anaconda. The trail heads south up Rock Creek, over the pass, and down the east side along the West Fork, LaMarche Creek tributary of the Big Hole River. This is the highest named pass along Montana's Great Divide.

41. Pintler Pass (8,738') — located in the heart of the Anaconda-Pintler Wilderness between East and West Pintler Peaks. From above the popular Johnson Lake, the trail climbs steeply to the head of the Falls Fork of Rock Creek and descends east of the Divide into the Pintler Creek tributary of the Big Hole River. It is named after Charles Pintler, an early-day miner-settler.

42. Gibbons Pass (6,982') — a historic pass south of Sula. West of the Divide, the old road leaves Highway 93 four miles south of Sula, crosses the timbered pass, and drops down Prairie and Trail Creeks to the Big Hole Valley near Wisdom. The pass was an obstacle to wagon teamsters as early as the late 1850s. It was named for General John Gibbon, whose soldiers suffered a humiliating defeat at the southeast foot of the pass in 1877 by Chief Joseph and his band of Nez Perce.

43. Chief Joseph Pass (7,264') — became Montana's most recently-named Continental Divide Pass in 1963, honoring the great Nez Perce leader. State Highway 43 climbs up Chief Joseph Creek to the pass from the Big Hole Battle-field National Monument, where Chief Joseph defeated Colonel Gibbon in 1877. From the 49th Parallel, which defines the northern border of Montana all the way to this point, both slopes of the Divide have fallen entirely within the State. Here, the Divide Range joins with the Bitterroot Range to form the Montana-Idaho line and continues south-southeast along the crest of the Bitterroots all the way to Raynolds Pass. This fascinating quirk of the Great Divide can be better appreciated when viewed from the opposite direction when, after following the summit of the Bitterroots for hundreds of miles, the Divide line veers sharply away from the range to the northeast along the top of the Anacondas.

44. Big Hole Pass (7,236') — a winding dirt road rises gently on the eastern (Montana) side of the Divide from the Big Hole Valley along Moose, Swamp, Pioneer, and Ruby Creeks dropping off sharply to Gibbonsville, Idaho, eight miles west of the pass. This pass is featured elsewhere in this *Geographic* in notes about early-day pioneer Leo Hagel and Big Hole Valley rancher Jack Hirschy.

45. Goldstone Pass (9,000') — located at the southern end of the West Big Hole roadless area at the headwaters of the Big Hole River and traversed only by a set of four-wheel-drive tracks. The pass sits near the head of Bloody Dick Creek. Cowbone Lake lies just below the pass on the Montana side. Around 1920 cattle were being driven over the Divide in late fall during a blinding storm that sent temperatures plummeting, heavy snow falling and the surface of the lake freezing with a thin sheet of ice. About 90 head of cattle fell through the ice to a watery grave. To this day their bones can be seen at the bottom of the lake.

46. Lemhi Pass (7,373') — the top of this historic pass is open grassland, which extends to the south in table-like plateaus. A good but winding gravel road ascends the east side (Montana) along Horse Prairie and Trail Creeks. Below the pass Horse Prairie Creek and the Red Rock River join to form the Beaverhead River. Captain Lewis finally reached the Pacific side of the Divide at this pass on August 12, 1805. Captain Clark and Sacajawea soon followed. The name is a corruption of Limhi, a figure in the Book of Mormon.

47. Bannock Pass (7,484') — a paved road follows an ancient trail from Armstead, Montana, up Horse Prairie and Divide Creeks over the top to Leadore, Idaho. Bannock is a Shoshonean word meaning "tuft of hair thrown from forehead." One of the oldest railroad companies in the United States, the Gilmore and Pittsburgh, built a 55-mile-long line from Armstead in 1910, crossing Bannock Pass by means of a 75' tunnel near the top. The railroad's historian, Thomas Taber, described the line as a railroad that " ... started from nowhere, traversed through nothing and ended up nowhere." It was actually part of a costly $6 million dream of some Northern Pacific officials to some day run the N.P.'s main line over Bannock Pass in order to avoid the rugged Montana-Idaho mountains west of Mullan Pass.

48. Medicine Lodge Pass (7,650') — from Dell, Montana, a gravel road runs up Sheep Creek over the top to Dubois, Idaho, by way of Medicine Lodge Creek. This age-old traverse was named for a 60-foot-high medicine lodge reputed to have been built in the area by Blackfeet Indians for ceremonies that would protect them in battle. Interestingly, the weathered sign at the top reads "Bannock

Top: *From Lemhi Pass looking east into Montana; Captain Lewis reached this Divide summit in August 1805.* Center: *Austere Divide landscape at Medicine Lodge Pass.* Bottom: *Red Rock Pass, the named pass closest to the most distant source of the Missouri River.* BILL CUNNINGHAM PHOTOS

Pass." Some called it Father's Defile after Father De Smet crossed it in 1841.

49. Monida Pass (6,823') — here the Divide forms the extreme southwestern boundary of Montana. All four lanes of I-15 make a long, fairly gentle climb to the top from the Red Rock River, south to Idaho Falls, Idaho. The almost deserted small town of Monida, Montana, was a stage stop on the trail from Salt Lake City to the Montana gold camps. When the Utah and Northern Railroad was built over the pass in 1880, a train dispatcher named the border station Monida, combining the names of Montana and Idaho.

50. Red Rock Pass (7,056') — from Henry's Lake, Idaho, a good gravel road crosses this gap on the eastern edge of the Centennial Mountains and drops into the headwaters of the Red Rock River in the expansive Centennial Valley of southwestern Montana. This is the named pass closest to the extreme source of the Missouri. In 1872 Hayden's men called it West Pass.

51. Squaw Pass (7,262') — this pass separates Duck Creek in the Snake River system from the Red Rock River in the Missouri drainage. The Bannock Indians often camped between the mouth of the larger Squaw Creek and the smaller Papoose Creek.

52. Raynolds Pass (6,836') — in high sagebrush flats and benches, U.S. Highway 87 climbs this pass from the Madison River below Quake Lake. Andrew Henry first crossed the pass in 1810. Later, the early trappers may have crossed here when they spoke of moving "through the North Pass to Missouri Lake in which rises the Madison Fork of the Missouri River." The pass wasn't named until Captain William F. Raynolds crossed it with Jim Bridger and reported on it in 1860.

53. Targhee Pass (7,072') — U.S. Route 20 climbs this ancient traverse along the South Fork of the Madison River and Denny Creek from West Yellowstone. It was named for Chief Tyghee of the Bannocks, who died in the 1870s. The main Bannock trail passed through this gap from the Snake River plains to the Gallatin Valley. In 1872 Hayden's surveyors proposed it for a railroad from Salt Lake City to Yellowstone Park.

54. Reas Pass (6,935') — only about four miles west of Yellowstone Park. The Union Pacific railroad crosses this forested pass from the Henry's Fork and down a branch of the Madison River to West Yellowstone, Montana. It is here that we conclude our long journey across 54 Continental Divide gates in Montana, from Brown Pass near the international boundary to Reas Pass on the edge of our country's oldest national park.

Right: *In 1984, the Bonneville Power Administration crossed Champion Pass with a 500 KV powerline connecting Colstrip Electric generating plants 3 and 4 in eastern Montana with the northwest power grid. This historic crossing is certainly one of the most significant industrial developments along the Continental Divide since the construction of the railroads.*

Left top: *On the Continental Divide south of Lembi Pass.*
Bottom: *Monida, Montana, a community practically on its namesake pass.*
Right top: *Rogers Pass.* Bottom: *On the Continental Divide south of Spotted Bear Pass.* BILL CUNNINGHAM PHOTOS

Mountain Ranges on Montana's Continental Divide

Where there are passes there are mountains, and where there are mountains in western Montana the Continental Divide is apt to be close by. Of the approximately 120 major ranges and subranges in Montana the following contain the Continent's dividing ridge (presented from north to south):

1. **Boundary Mountains** — a small group of mountains along the northern border of Glacier Park branching west of the Divide north of Kintla Lake.

2. **Lewis Range** — named by Meriwether Lewis, this is the 65-mile-long main crest of Glacier Park, the highest summit of which is 10,466' Mt. Cleveland.

3. **Hudson Bay Divide** — an offshoot from the Continental Divide at Triple Divide Peak in Glacier Park, trending northeast and separating the waters of Hudson Bay from those draining into the Atlantic Ocean via the Gulf of Mexico.

4. **Continental Divide Range** — an unofficial name for the Continental Divide mountains that extend through the Bob Marshall Country from Marias Pass south to Rogers Pass.

5. **Flathead Alps** — located in the southern portion of the Bob Marshall Wilderness, this subrange begins at Junction Mountain on the Continental Divide and extends westward toward the South Fork of the Flathead River.

6. **Robert E. Lee Range** — Some 30 years ago this unofficial name was given to the Continental Divide mountains south of Rogers Pass in the vicinity of Stemple Pass in an unsuccessful effort to name some Montana ranges after famous historical figures. The range includes the Nevada Mountains between Stemple Pass and Mullan Pass.

7. **Deer Lodge Mountains** (also called Boulder Mountains) — an uncommon name for the mountains that run from Avon south to Butte, which includes the Electric Peak/Thunderbolt Mountain area along the Divide.

8. **Highland Mountains** — a small range of 10,000-foot peaks just south of Butte; the highest summit is 10,223' Table Mountain, which is a few miles south of the Divide.

9. **Anaconda Range** — a rugged stretch of the Divide southwest of Anaconda, for which it is named. Most of the range is within the Anaconda-Pintler Wilderness. The loftiest summit is 10,793' West Goat Peak.

10. Pintler Range — applies to the western extension of the Anaconda Range above the Big Hole Valley; it was named after early-day Big Hole rancher Charles Pintler.

11. Bitterroot Range — the longest range in Montana, stretching some 450 miles from Lookout Pass south to Raynolds Pass. As the boundary between Montana and Idaho it is the most rugged border between any two states, and the only interstate boundary that runs along the Continenal Divide. The Continental Divide follows the crest of the Bitterroots north until reaching a timbered hill just north of Chief Joseph Pass, at which point it suddenly veers away from the Bitterroot Range heading northeast along the crest of the Pintlars. The northern portion of the Bitterroots away from the Continental Divide is generally considered to be the "main" Bitterroot, named after Montana's official state flower. South of Chief Joseph Pass where the high crest of the Bitterroot Range forms the Continental Divide are five distinct subranges, with the Beaverhead Range encompassing the first four. They are as follows:

Beaverhead Range — runs for 165 miles along the Divide from Chief Joseph Pass south to Monida Pass encompassing the West Big Hole, Italian Peaks, Lima Peaks, and Red Conglomerate subranges. The name comes from Beaverhead Rock which was dubbed by Lewis and Clark as they traveled up the Beaverhead River in 1805.

West Big Hole Mountains — extend for 55 miles from Chief Joseph Pass south to Lemhi Pass. The crest of the Divide consists of beautiful alpine peaks above 10,000 feet with the highest summit in the range being 10,621' Homer Youngs Peak just east of the Continental Divide.

Italian Peaks — located in the extreme southwest "hidden" corner of the state, this remote range contains the only peaks above 11,000' on Montana's Continental Divide.

Lima Peaks — also called Garfield Peaks, these open, grassy 10,000' mountains are immediately northwest of Monida Pass.

Red Conglomerate Peaks — a series of 10,000' peaks on the Continental Divide just west of Monida Pass, which form the southern portion of the Lima Peaks complex.

Centennial Mountains — a 50-mile-long, east-west expanse of rugged mountains and grassy plateaus running from Monida Pass east to Red Rock Pass. They are particularly distinctive for their abrupt northern

The highest peaks along Montana's Continental Divide are found in the Italian Peaks—Montana's "hidden corner." BRUCE SELYEM

escarpment that rises 3,000 to 4,000' above Montana's Red Rock Lakes/Centennial Valley.

12. Henry's Lake Mountains — a semi-circle of 10,000' peaks along the Divide north of Henry's Lake, Idaho. This poorly-defined range phases into portions of the nearby Centennial and Madison Ranges.

Lionhead Mountains — a subrange and highest portion of the Henry's Lake Mountains just west of West

Yellowstone between Raynolds and Targhee Passes. The Lionhead contains several 10,000'-plus peaks along the Continental Divide.

13. Yellowstone Rockies — refers to the Middle Rockies ranges surrounding Yellowstone National Park. The broad, heavily-forested plateau of the Continental Divide as it leaves Montana inside Yellowstone Park at the intersection of Montana, Idaho and Wyoming is actually part of the headwaters of the South Fork of the Madison River.

PART IV

Wilderness:
The Essence of the Divide

Born on the Continental Divide, the Middle Fork of the Flathead River, in one of its more restful moods, is the lifeline of the Great Bear Wilderness. LARRY MAYER

Wilderness Areas—
Wilderness with a Big "W"

It struck me while hiking alone this past summer atop a vast tundra plateau near the top of a majestic Continental Divide summit — Scapegoat Mountain — in the heart of its namesake wilderness. A dominant feature of much of Montana's 800-mile-long serpentine segment of the Divide is its relative remoteness and wildness. The myriad primeval, undeveloped basins dropping off from the Divide create a mood of excitement that can bring out the explorer in us, whether we actually trek the rugged crest or simply want to know that much of our nation's backbone survives as the early-day explorers first encountered it.

Significant stretches of Montana's Divide country have thus far escaped exploitation largely because of the geographical accident of isolation from population and economic markets. Spurred by this good fortune, citizen conservationists have worked effectively for more than half a century to save remnants of Montana's Great Divide wilderness. The results, in addition to the million-acre wilderness gem of Glacier National Park, are five designated wildernesses that touch or straddle Montana's Continental Divide.

When Lewis and Clark explored the vast land we now call Montana, they encountered a wilderness of some 93 million acres. Today, scarcely a tenth of this land remains wild and undisturbed. And much of the surviving wild country clings to the most isolated reaches of the Great Divide. As such, wilderness and its dominant topographical feature — the Continental Divide — intertwine so as to form the heart and soul of Montana.

There are many definitions and perspectives concerning wilderness. But in 1964 Congress defined the term to mean an area of undeveloped federal land set aside for enduring preservation in its natural state. In many ways, the protection of wildland is the ultimate expression of human humility toward the earth and its inhabitants. I have seen grizzly bears, mountain goats and trumpeter swans in wild country along or near the Great Divide and I am reminded that these species simply cannot live close to people. Wilderness is for their benefit as well as ours. I have seen the stress and anxiety of urban-bound people evaporate from their faces and minds as they've wandered the crest of the Chinese Wall. That, I would not trade for anything.

From north to south we will look at wilderness from Glacier Park to the northwestern edge of Yellowstone.

1. Glacier National Park — The Glacier back country is the epitome of high Divide wilderness in its most spectacular form. This "land of shining mountains" was molded by fire, torrential rains, internal pressures and the great continental ice sheets to produce a million-acre wilderness with more than 200 gemlike lakes, countless waterfalls, vertical relief of thousands of feet, and broad U-shaped valleys. The Continental Divide separates the park into two nearly equal parts and is itself bisected by a road in only one location, at Logan Pass. Upon this jagged and varied landscape exist some 1,200 plant species, at least 200 kinds of birds and about 60 mammals, some of which need the security and isolation of wilderness. The variety of the flora and fauna results from the five life zones that occur in Glacier. From the equivalent of polar ice and snow high along the Divide, one can descend into alpine tundra, coniferous forest, deciduous forest and grassland. Although protected as a national park, Glacier has not yet been added to our nation's wilderness system by Congress.

1. The Bob Marshall Wilderness Complex — consists of the contiguous 1.5-million-acre Great Bear, Bob Marshall and Scapegoat wilderness areas plus nearly one million acres of unprotected wild country that resembles a giant horseshoe around the designated wilderness. Based on distance between roads, the Bob Marshall country from Marias Pass south to Rogers Pass is Montana's wildest and most remote segment of the Divide. Between these two points are some 140 air miles through which more than 200 surface miles of roadless Divide drops, rises and winds. Spreading from the windswept Divide are deep limestone canyons, immense cliffs, old-growth forests, rushing rivers, lush subalpine basins, and broad river valleys with prairie-like parks. This diverse land is home to almost every big game species living in North America, including the threatened grizzly bear, endangered Rocky Mountain wolf and many more common species such as deer, elk, moose, bighorn sheep and mountain goats. Although the peaks along the Divide here are not the loftiest ones in the "Bob," Scapegoat Mountain at 9,204' is the fifth highest peak in the complex. On the north end, the four-mile-long limestone wall of Corrugate Ridge is a distinctive Divide landmark. Farther south the Divide is dominated by the 13-mile-long, 1,000' limestone escarpment of the famed Chinese Wall. This classic overthrust formation climbs gradually out of the west from the White River only to drop abruptly into the lush subalpine meadows on the east side.

2. Great Bear Wilderness — 285,000 acres — encompasses the entire upper drainage of the wild, free-flowing Middle Fork of the Flathead River from the

Here the Continental Divide rises to over 9,000' to form majestic plateaus on the southeastern flank of Scapegoat Mountain. BILL CUNNINGHAM

Continental Divide westward to the rugged peaks of the Flathead Range. Topography varies from knifelike ridgetops along the Divide, to gentle-sloping alpine meadows, to steeply timbered mountainsides, to open river-bottom parks. Glacial action, which created U-shaped valleys and glacial cirques along the Divide, largely determined the topography and drainage patterns of the Great Bear.

The Middle Fork of the Flathead is regarded as Montana's wildest river. Old timers called it Big River and the trail that parallels it still goes by that name. The Big River begins modestly as a drop of melting snow atop the Continental Divide on the steep slope of a mountain where a glacier once rode the landscape. Joining with other drops to

become a tiny rivulet it tumbles down hillsides and seeps through spruce bogs and subalpine meadows. Countless other tributaries merge to enter the main channel of the Big River on its journey to the Pacific. This lifeline of a great wilderness watershed is a river of constantly changing moods, from placid emerald pools so clear that the spots can be counted on the backs of native cutthroat to frenzied rushes of white foam hellbent for the mighty Columbia. A note of interest is that a high elevation game-drive site used by prehistoric man during the "forager" period some 5,000 years ago has been identified on the Continental Divide near the headwaters of the Middle Fork.

3. Bob Marshall Wilderness — 1,009,000 acres — the most remote part of the "Bob" is the spine of the Great Divide —the heart of which is the Chinese Wall. The Divide serves as a climatic barrier, which, in turn, influences vegetation, wildlife and the character of this primitive land itself. Major streams emanate from the Divide in the Bob Marshall, including the blue-ribbon South Fork of the Flathead, which gets its start from the remote Danaher Basin. East of the Divide is the vast Sun River drainage. The western portion of the Sun River country is included in a 200,000-acre game preserve, which the Montana legislature closed to hunting in 1912 to maintain the huge, aboriginal Sun River elk herd of some 3,000 animals. Indeed, the basins on both sides of the Divide are classic wilderness elk country. It is also grizzly country, and these magnificent wilderness-dependent animals amble along or near the Divide in search of wild parsnips, marmots and other tasty morsels. To me, the ultimate wilderness experience is to see a wild grizzly in wild country along the spine of the "Bob" in a setting such as the Wall Creek Cliffs or the Chinese Wall. Memories of the highest, most remote reaches of the Bob Marshall country along the Great Divide are enriched by such priceless sightings.

4. Scapegoat Wilderness — This 240,000-acre wilderness is a contiguous part of the Bob Marshall complex. During the 1960s Forest Service plans to build a road over the Divide near Scapegoat Mountain (9,204') brought a storm of citizen protest that eventually led to wilderness designation of the area in 1972. The wilderness straddles both sides of the Continental Divide, forming the headwaters of the Dearborn River and Falls Creek drainages on the east side and of various forks of the Big Blackfoot River to the west. The massive limestone cliffs of Scapegoat Mountain, which extend more than three miles on the east face in a series of amphitheaters, are an extension of the Chinese Wall formation. The scattered subalpine forests and open parks below Scapegoat at the

Meadows, timber and peaks—the essence of the Great Divide as it rises to the rocky summit of Electric Peak in the Anaconda-Pintler Wilderness. RON GLOVAN

heads of the Dearborn, Halfmoon Park and the Green Fork are made even more beautiful by the rough-hewn signatures of old burns. During the summer the base of the Divide is alive with fireweed, beargrass and numerous other flowering plants. Most of the 14 lakes and 89 miles of streams in the Scapegoat Wilderness are fishable for cutthroat and rainbow trout. The up-and-down, serpentine nature of Montana's Continental Divide is more evident from the top of Scapegoat Mountain than from anywhere else I've been along the Divide.

5. Anaconda-Pintler Wilderness — the Anaconda Range of southwestern Montana contains some of the wildest, most scenic Continental Divide country to be found anywhere. The 158,516-acre Anaconda-Pintler Wilderness occupies the heart of this rugged 40-mile, east-west expanse of the Great Divide. Although lacking some life zones found on lower elevations, the wilderness does contain a wide array of topography and vegetation. This diversity is displayed by the broad range of low willow flats along the East Fork on the Bitterroot River on the west end all the way up to the high point in the range — West Goat Peak (10,793'). The classic signatures of past glaciation dominate the Divide. Nearly a vertical mile separates the top of the Divide from the lowlands. Natural wildland diversity also is reflected by the more than two dozen native mammals, including wolverine, lynx, mountain lion and flying squirrel. The wilderness provides the headwaters of the some of the world's finest trout streams: Rock Creek and branches of the Bitterroot and Big Hole rivers. Spectacular cirques with dozens of alpine lakes, U-shaped valleys and glacial moraines combine to form a wilderness wonderland along the Divide. Perpetual snowbanks along the crest feed sparkling streams that tumble down steep canyons. The "Hi-Line" trail along and near the Continental Divide offers stupendous, panoramic views of the expansive Big Hole Valley and many distant mountain ranges.

6. Red Rock Lakes Wilderness — is located in the wide-open landscape of extreme southwest Montana's Centennial Valley near the northwest corner of Yellowstone Park. This virtually undeveloped valley, crossed only by gravel roads, is dominated by an amazing system of interconnecting marshes and waterways. The more than 14,000 acres of wetlands provide irreplaceable habitat and solitude for a stunning array of birds and other wildlife. The flat marshlands of the valley give way to the rolling foothills of the Gravelly Range to the north and to the majestic Continental Divide uplift of the Centennial Range. The center of the valley is occupied by the 40,300-acre Red Rock Lakes National Wildlife Refuge administered

The Red Rock Lakes Wilderness begins in the marshlands of 6,600' Centennial Valley and ascends some 3,000 vertical feet to the crest of the Centennial Range. JOHN REDDY

by the U.S. Fish and Wildlife Service. Located within the core of the refuge is the 32,350-acre Red Rock Lakes Wilderness, which was designated by Congress in 1976. The refuge was established in 1935 to safeguard the rare trumpeter swan, largest of all North American waterfowl, and is best known for its birdlife. Some 215 species of birds have been found within this wetlands wilderness including 23 kinds of ducks and geese along with a myriad of shorebirds, sora rails, peregrine falcons and bald and golden eagles. The large, shallow Upper and Lower Red Rock Lakes are actually remnants of an ancient and larger lake. Over the millenia the valley has gradually filled with alluvium. As this slow process continues, sedimentation eventually will extinguish the lakes. Moose are year-round residents in the wilderness, with elk, deer and pronghorn antelope living on the refuge wilderness during every season except winter. Snowfall averages about 150 inches annually, and frost usually occurs in every month of the year. This part of Montana has the longest winters in the continental United States.

Wildlands Education along the Great Divide

During the hot, dry, early summer of 1985, as I was exploring segments of the Divide for this book, I was privileged to instruct a wilderness field course for university students. The program was sponsored by the Wildlands Research Institute under the auspices of San Francisco State University. The students were from all over the United States and their "classrooms" for most of the 2½ weeks we shared were a few of the unprotected wild stretches of Montana's Divide country: Falls Creek/Silver King; Nevada Mountain, Electric Peak, the North Big Hole and the West Big Hole. Within this living environment, and along the lonely windswept ridges of the nation's backbone, we learned together as we opened our senses to the enduring values of wild country. Our topics of discussion along the Divide ranged from wilderness politics to wilderness ecology. We could have covered the same subjects in an indoor classroom, but the experience meant more to each of us as we learned about wildland issues out on the lands that have continued to spark

Top: *Within the North Big Hole roadless area, Big Hole rancher Jim Welch describes a controversial U.S. Forest Service timber-sale proposal to a group of Wildlands Research Institute students.* Bottom: *Students examine a new road built in Helena National Forest's Electric Peak roadless area for the Bison Mountain timber sale.* BILL CUNNINGHAM PHOTOS

controversy. The importance of preserving representative samples of Montana's Great Divide country for their educational value alone cannot be measured or over-estimated. The freedom, remoteness and wildness of the Continental Divide excites the mind, laying the groundwork for answers to questions we haven't even learned to ask.

Proposed Wilderness Areas— Wilderness with a Small W

Expressing alarm over the rapid loss of wild country, pioneer conservationist Robert Marshall, after whom the Bob Marshall Wilderness was named, noted that wilderness, even a half century ago, was "disappearing like a snowbank on a hot June day." Over the years Montana conservationists have advanced a wilderness protection proposal that, if adopted by Congress, would at least take the heat lamp off our melting snowbank. The Continental Divide portion of this proposal consists of additions to three existing wildernesses along with five separate wild areas.

1. **Rocky Mountain Front-Continental Divide** additions to the Bob Marshall Wilderness complex — along the wild, windswept Rocky Mountain Front, where mountains meet the plains, are nearly one-half million acres of unprotected wilderness adjoining the Great Bear, Bob Marshall and Scapegoat wildernesses. Protection of this corrugated land is vital to abundant wildlife populations: thousands of deer and elk, the nation's largest native population of Rocky Mountain bighorn sheep, mountain goats, perhaps 100 grizzlies, as well as black bears, mountain lions, moose and the endangered Rocky Mountain wolf. These east-side additions to the "Bob" proposed by conservation groups, such as the Bob Marshall Alliance, total about 320,000 acres of prime wildlands that have been used as wilderness for generations. Two of these additions abut the Continental Divide: Badger/Two Medicine on the north and Falls Creek/Silver King to the south.

Badger/Two Medicine — the southern and western boundaries of this extensive roadless area on the Lewis and Clark Forest are defined by the Divide. It is a forgotten land because visitors are attracted to the better-known Great Bear and Bob Marshall wildernesses and nearby Glacier Park. Here we find an inviting combination of rugged peaks, deep forest, clear streams, aspen thickets and fescue parks. This wild area has a unique combination of moist riparian and key big game habitat that are especially vital to the survival of the grizzly bear and wolf. This area was once part of the Blackfeet Reservation, and treaty agreements provide the Blackfeet with hunting, fishing and domestic wood-cutting rights. Wilderness designation of the 93,000-acre Badger/Two Medicine area depends largely on the ability of local conservationists to reach agreement with the Blackfeet Tribal Council.

Top: *Sunset on proposed Rocky Mountain Front additions to the Bob Marshall Wilderness—east slopes of the Continental Divide.* LARRY MAYER

Bottom: *Notch Peak defines a grand section in the Anaconda-Pintler Wilderness.* RON GLOVAN

Above: *At the foot of the Great Divide in the Danaher Basin, Bob Marshall Wilderness Guard Jerry Hess manties up a load to be transported by mule from Basin Creek to Big Prairie. Jerry is one of a dedicated breed of on-the-ground Wilderness rangers who believe that educating people about minimum-impact camping is far more effective than regulating. He travels at least 1,500 miles a year along the western slopes of the Continental Divide in the Bob contacting visitors, maintaining patrol cabins along with some 600 miles of trails, fixing phone lines and helping with rescue missions. Living for five to six months a year in the 450,000 wilderness acres that he and two other back-country rangers patrol has a humbling effect on Jerry. A trip up Haystack Mountain on the Chinese Wall four years ago, during his first season in the Bob, left a lasting impression. "It really gave me a sense of being on the Divide—like being in God's country," he said. "It is a special place."* BILL CUNNINGHAM

101

Falls Creek/Silver King — (82,000 acres) — Some 90 miles to the south lies some unprotected roadless country between the Wood-Ford Creek road south to the Continental Divide and onto historic Lewis and Clark Pass. This addition includes the spectacular limestone canyon of Devil's Glen on the wilderness waterway of the Dearborn — a river of ever-changing sights from clear deep pools to foaming waterfalls. Farther south, the vast Falls Creek watershed begins on the Divide on both sides of 8,773' Caribou Peak. Just west of the Divide is the undisturbed upper Alice Creek Basin — a pleasing contrast to the higher Divide ridges to the north.

2. **Nevada Mountain** (50,400 acres) — Located between Lincoln and Helena, Nevada Mountain is the largest unprotected roadless area on the Helena National Forest and it straddles the Divide for 15 miles. The more prominent geographical features are Nevada and Black Mountains — each rising above 8,000'. The heads of drainages along the Divide are characterized by scenic rocky cirques, especially on the east side. The country west of the Divide consists of steep, densely-forested finger ridges with numerous parks on the south-facing slopes. As such, the habitat is ideal for some 1,000 elk and nearly as many deer. Heavy roading and logging on all sides of the area make the thick stands of small lodgepole pine even more important as elk security cover during the fall hunting season. Because of deep snowpack and the numerous streams that head up along the Divide, the Nevada Mountain area is an important producer of pure water for downstream users in the Little Prickly Pear Creek, Nevada Creek and Blackfoot River drainages.

3. **Electric Peak/Blackfoot Meadows** — (43,500 acres) — Nearly 13 miles of the Great Divide wind through this wildlife-rich roadless area shared by the Helena and Deerlodge National Forests between Helena and Butte. The high point along the Divide is 8,597' Thunderbolt Mountain, with nearby Electric Peak rising to 8,340'. Once in a while grizzly bears use this country. A large boar was mistakenly shot in the area near the Divide in the early 1980s. On the Columbia side of the Divide countless small streams, springs and groundwater seeps join to form picturesque Blackfoot Meadows in the heart of the area, "land of 1,000 beaver ponds." On the Missouri side, Cottonwood Lake is the most prominent feature. The lake is nestled at the base of a mile-long subalpine meadow, which stretches north toward the rugged slopes of the Divide and is used heavily by summering elk.

4. **Additions to the Anaconda-Pintler Wilderness** —The A-P is surrounded by about 84,000 acres of unprotected

First light sets the Great Divide aglow along the summit of the proposed West Big Hole Wilderness. BILL CUNNINGHAM

national forest wildlands. As the portals to the higher country, these adjacent roadless areas have been used as wilderness for generations. They provide irreplaceable wildlife security habitat, old-growth forests and a pleasing recreational contrast to the "goat rocks" above. To help round out the wilderness boundary, conservationists are proposing about 56,000 acres of additions:

Northeast Additions (19,100 acres) — Lofty Mt. Evans (10,641') atop the Great Divide is in the heart of the beautiful Storm Lake addition. This classic alpine setting includes more than three dozen glittering tarns surrounded by the craggy peaks of the Divide. Farther west the lovely 100-acre Meadow and Dexter Basin would be added so as to add depth and diversity to the northern boundary.

Southwest Additions — North Big Hole — (37,000 acres) — This area contains major tributaries to the famed blue-ribbon Big Hole River, such as Plimpton, Thompson, Howell and McCormick Creeks. Each of these south-facing valleys is marked with well-defined terminal moraines at its mouth. Vegetative cover is mostly forest, with dense thickets of small-diameter lodgepole pine predominating. The bottoms are typically open meadow and willow with slow, meandering streams, giving way to aspen and spruce higher up. The wildlife diversity of this country is truly astonishing. An unclassified species of unusual freshwater clams lives in a tiny stream flowing through Clam Valley in the heart of the proposed addition. The area along the adjoining private land boundary is especially important for elk calving, supporting a herd numbering in the hundreds. Outstanding scenic and cultural features of the North Big Hole include rock spires, historic rifle pits and probable Indian relics.

5. **West Big Hole** (86,000 acres) — Conservationists have long proposed protection against roads and logging in the higher and middle slopes of this Continental Divide wild country. Rising from the sunset side of the expansive Big Hole River Valley west of Wisdom and Jackson, the snowy southern Bitterroot Mountains reach over 10,000' along the Divide before dropping sharply into Idaho. Above the Big Hole Valley's sagebrush-covered plains, the foothills of the West Big Hole rise gradually, merging into glaciated U-shaped canyons and finally jutting sharply to the Great Divide. Along the Montana side of the Divide are nestled some 25 jewel-like alpine lakes, many with good populations of trout. Despite the ruggedness and remoteness of this area, it is surprisingly accessible to family back-country recreation. The lower elevation streams and lush meadows are an absolute delight for hiking, camping and fishing. Wildlife are as diverse as the landscape, with black bear, mountain lion, elk, deer, moose, goats and wolverine. The rare arctic grayling occurs in some of the lakes and streams. This high country is one of the Beaverhead Forest's best water producers, providing abundant flows of quality water for Butte, ranchers and other downstream users.

6. **Italian Peaks** (52,000 acres) — Located in Montana's "hidden corner" at the state's southernmost extremity, the area is dominated by 10,998' Italian Peak — a Divide peak containing a sheer 2,000' precipice of shattered limestone. The Divide forms the southern and western boundaries of this remote, windblown region. North of Italian Peak is 11,141 Eighteenmile Peak — the highest point on the Continental Divide between Alberta's Banff Park and the

Wind River Range in Wyoming. Most of the area is either above timberline or interspersed with scattered patches of whitebark and lodgepole pines. This high, open country provides habitat for mountain goats, summer range for elk, and refuge for many smaller mammals. It also may be habitat for the transitory, endangered gray wolf.

7. Centennial Mountains (92,000 acres) — The rugged Centennials straddle the Divide on the western edge of the greater Yellowstone ecosystem between Montana and Idaho. The Bureau of Land Management and the Forest Service are conducting a joint wilderness study for 72,230 acres in the two states. Conservationists are urging more comprehensive protection to include qualified contiguous lands. This Divide range is one of the few in the northern Rockies that trend east-west. The northern face rises more than 3,000' in less than one mile from the already high 6,600' Centennial Valley. The western Centennials display a variety of earthflows and landslides. The heavy snowpack on the Montana side drains into the Red Rock River. Throughout the area there are grasslands, meadows and parks, sagebrush-grasslands, aspen stands and some alpine and subalpine areas within and near the U.S. Sheep Experiment Station along the Divide. The severe winter climate prevents wintering by most big game species except for bear, moose and elk in the extreme western portion. The Centennials are home to an important interstate elk herd of some 300 to 500 animals. Moose also migrate across the high Divide. The area is important grizzly bear habitat when viewed within the context of the Yellowstone population. Wolves also have been sighted in the Centennials as recently as the 1970s. This wildland too is essential to the recovery of the endangered peregrine falcon. One of the Continent's few relict native grayling populations inhabits Upper Red Rock Lake on the adjoining refuge wilderness. This wild 35-mile-long stretch of the Divide is the watershed for the rich marsh ecosystem of the adjoining Red Rock Lakes Refuge and Wilderness. Development on the steep, unstable soils of the northern slopes of the Centennials could lead to increased siltation of refuge waters. Already, accelerated erosion is occurring from past sheep grazing at the head of Odell Creek and from past phosphate mining. This proposed wilderness encompasses the source of the Missouri River most distant from its mouth —the headwaters of secluded Hellroaring Creek.

8. Lionhead (30,200 acres) — This Gallatin Forest wild area straddles the Continental Divide for 10½ miles between Montana and Idaho just west of West Yellowstone. The most rugged and remote of the Henry's Lake

The 10,000' Continental Divide ridge towers above the Rock Island Lake Basin in the heart of the West Big Hole country. BRUCE SELYEM

Mountains, the steep slopes of the Lionhead range from 6,400' along the Madison River to the summit of Sheep Point at 10,609'. The area has an unusually high concentration of high peaks in a small perimeter along the Divide. Nine subalpine lakes are hidden in several cirque basins with 15-acre Coffin Lake being the largest and most popular. This segment of the Divide is the headwaters of four major undisturbed tributaries to the Madison River. Geologically, these mountains consist of blocks of limestone sitting atop layers of shale and Yellowstone Park volcanics. The Lionhead is occupied grizzly bear habitat as well as summer and winter range for elk, moose, deer and bighorn sheep. Ospreys and bald eagles also live along the northern reaches of the area near Earthquake Lake.

Continental Divide Wildlands— An Uncertain Future

The above-described remnants of unprotected Great Divide wild country are scattered like a string of pearls from Glacier to Yellowstone Parks. All or portions of each of these eight areas or clusters of areas are being considered for possible wilderness designation by Congress. At the same time, the U.S. Forest Service has embarked on a long-range planning effort wherein each of the 10 national forests in Montana has produced a tentative Forest Plan that will guide land management for the next 50 years. Six of these Forest Plans contain draft plans for seven of the "small w" wildernesses described above. If Congress does not enact a Montana wilderness bill, the following summaries of proposed Forest Service management foretell what may happen to the last unprotected vestiges of wildness along Montana's Great Divide.

1. **Rocky Mountain Front** additions to the Bob Marshall Wilderness Complex:

Badger/Two Medicine — This entire 102,000-acre roadless area has been leased for oil and gas exploration, and at least one drilling permit already has been applied for in Hall Creek, only three miles south of Glacier Park. Even though the draft Forest Plan would set aside 84,846 acres as "roadless," roads for mineral exploration and other uses still could be built. About 4,527 acres in the north end of this remote wildlife sanctuary would be roaded and logged under the Lewis and Clark Forest Plan.

Falls Creeks/Silver King — The Lewis and Clark Forest Plan recommends that 22,660 acres be added to the Scapegoat Wilderness. An additional 43,078 acres would remain "roadless" unless oil and gas exploratory roads are developed into such presently wild enclaves as the Dearborn and Falls Creek drainages. The northern portion of the area is leased for oil and gas. About 2,137 acres are in the timber base, which could mean roads into the upper reaches of Petty, Moudess and Elk Creeks on the high Scapegoat boundary. The Helena Forest portion of the area west of the Divide is recommended for a combination of roadless and minimum-level management. Still, the upper Alice Creek basin has been leased so development could occur in the future without wilderness designation.

2. **Nevada Mountain** —about 15,000 acres of this 50,000-acre roadless area are proposed for logging in the draft Helena Forest Plan. The only logging actually on the Divide

Top: *Heavily timbered western slopes of the Divide contrast sharply with rocky cliffs and headwalls on the east side of proposed Nevada Mountain Wilderness. The view here is to the north from Black Mountain.* Bottom: *Large-scale clearcut logging of lodgepole pine in the West Big Hole. Here in Big Swamp Creek development meets wilderness under the crest of the Divide.* BILL CUNNINGHAM PHOTOS

would occur just northeast of Black Mountain. Four timber sales are scheduled during the next decade, which would result in about 1,000 acres being cut for 6.5 million board feet of timber with 13 miles of new roads. Meanwhile, most of the area has been leased for oil and gas exploration, with the industry calling the potential for discovery moderate. Some portions of the area have been impacted by placer mining, such as the head of Nevada Creek just west of the Divide.

3. Electric Peak/Blackfoot Meadows — On the Helena Forest side (west of the Divide) more than 7,000 acres of the roadless area are slated for roads and logging, mostly on the northern and eastern edges. The core of the area in scenic Blackfoot Meadows would be managed for nonmotorized roadless recreation, although some 41,848 acres of the area are blanketed by oil and gas leases. There are also 53 hardrock mining claims in the roadless area but the potential for development is thought to be low. The Deerlodge Forest also proposed some roadless nonmotorized management on its side of the Divide. However, about 2,500 roadless acres just north of Sugarloaf Mountain are in the timber base.

4. Anaconda-Pintler Wilderness Additions:

Northeast Corner — the Deerlodge Plan recommends a small, 4,114-acre Storm Lake Wilderness addition with most of the remaining area being in a complementary roadless allocation. The plan calls for some logging just below Dexter Basin to the west, which falls within the conservationist wilderness proposal.

Southwest Corner — the most serious impact to the North Big Hole addition is the Howell Creek timber sale which the Beaverhead Forest has scheduled for 1988. In 1981-1982 the Forest Service built a 10-mile-long road from Pintler Creek west to Clam Valley for access to the timber. At present the sale is pending because of strong local opposition. The Forest Plan recommends 6,571 acres in the rocky upper Hellroaring Creek drainage as wilderness. An additional 9,000 acres near Clam Valley would be roaded and logged under the draft Beaverhead Plan.

5. West Big Hole — the Beaverhead Plan recommends a high elevation 55,014-acre wilderness along the crest of the Continental Divide. About 14,000 acres in the larger conservationist wilderness proposal would be roaded and logged, most of which would be north of the glaciated Little Lake Creek drainage. The plan calls for a small but significant recreation area centered around Little Lake Creek but acknowledges that there is no guarantee against future roading.

Above: *The Divide forms the head of Alice Creek Basin—part of proposed Falls Creek/Silver King addition to Scapegoat Wilderness.* BILL CUNNINGHAM
Left: *Extensive helicopter-borne seismic exploration for oil and gas has occurred near the Divide in the proposed Badger/Two Medicine addition to the Bob.* BRUCE SELYEM

6. Italian Peaks — the draft Beaverhead Plan recommends a 12,907-acre wilderness next to the Divide, with forms of management in the rest of the area that would not normally require roads. Some of the proposed wilderness has been leased for oil and gas exploration with protective stipulations.

7. Lionhead — the draft Gallatin Forest Plan proposes a wilderness of 22,811 acres. The remaining 10,000 acres of the roadless area would include roads and logging on the eastern border near Watkins and Trapper Creek close to the Divide and manipulation of winter range for wildlife on the west side.

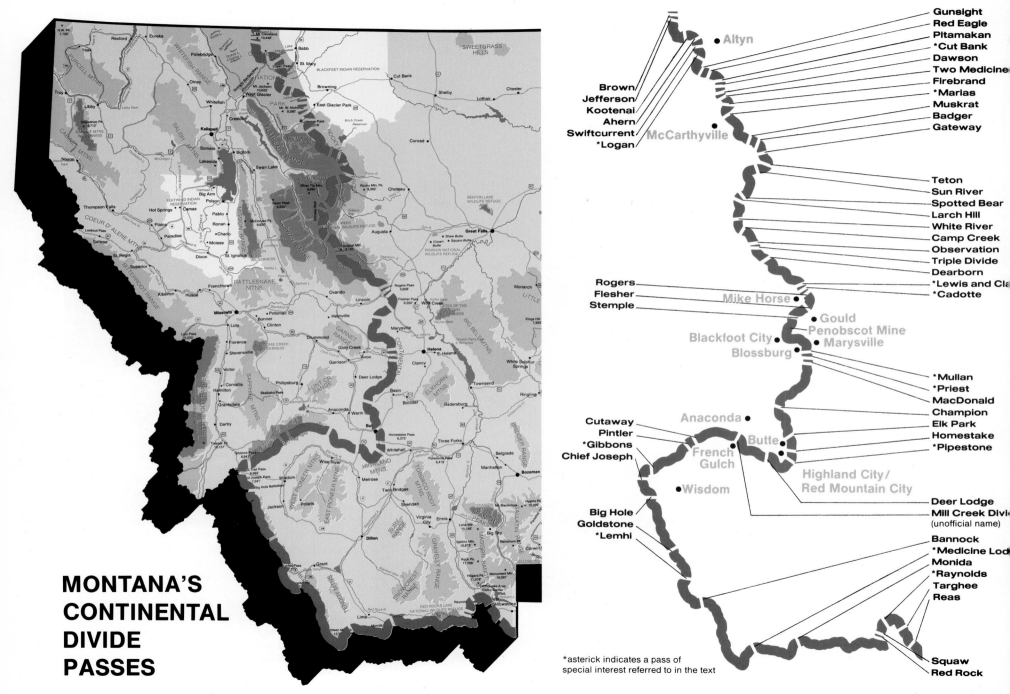

MONTANA'S CONTINENTAL DIVIDE PASSES

Gunsight
Red Eagle
Pitamakan
*Cut Bank
Dawson
Two Medicine
Firebrand
*Marias
Muskrat
Badger
Gateway

Brown
Jefferson
Kootenai
Ahern
Swiftcurrent
*Logan

Teton
Sun River
Spotted Bear
Larch Hill
White River
Camp Creek
Observation
Triple Divide
Dearborn
*Lewis and Cla
*Cadotte

Rogers
Flesher
Stemple

Gould
Penobscot Mine
Marysville
Blackfoot City
Blossburg

*Mullan
*Priest
MacDonald
Champion
Elk Park
Homestake
*Pipestone

Cutaway
Pintler
*Gibbons
Chief Joseph

Deer Lodge
Mill Creek Divi
(unofficial name)

Big Hole
Goldstone
*Lemhi

Bannock
*Medicine Lod
Monida
*Raynolds
Targhee
Reas

Squaw
Red Rock

*asterick indicates a pass of
special interest referred to in the text

106

KEY HISTORICAL POINTS

KEY GEOGRAPHICAL POINTS

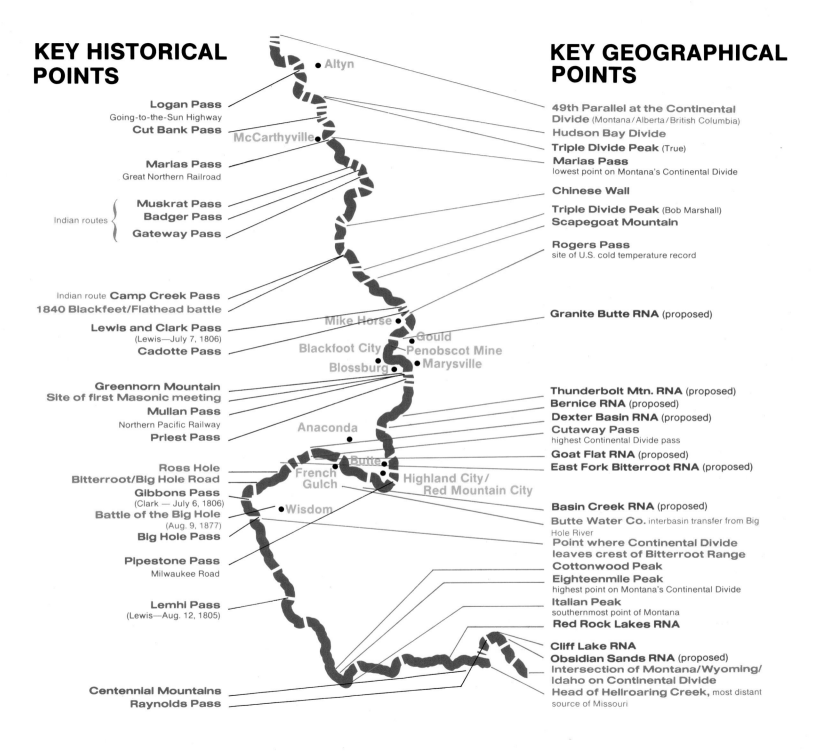

Logan Pass
Going-to-the-Sun Highway
Cut Bank Pass

Marias Pass
Great Northern Railroad

Indian routes {
Muskrat Pass
Badger Pass
Gateway Pass
}

Indian route **Camp Creek Pass**
1840 Blackfeet/Flathead battle

Lewis and Clark Pass
(Lewis—July 7, 1806)
Cadotte Pass

Greennorn Mountain
Site of first Masonic meeting
Mullan Pass
Northern Pacific Railway
Priest Pass

Ross Hole
Bitterroot/Big Hole Road
Gibbons Pass
(Clark — July 6, 1806)
Battle of the Big Hole
(Aug. 9, 1877)
Big Hole Pass

Pipestone Pass
Milwaukee Road

Lemhi Pass
(Lewis—Aug. 12, 1805)

Centennial Mountains
Raynolds Pass

Altyn
McCarthyville
Mike Horse
Gould
Blackfoot City
Penobscot Mine
Blossburg
Marysville
Anaconda
Butte
French
Gulch
Highland City/
Red Mountain City
Wisdom

49th Parallel at the Continental Divide (Montana/Alberta/British Columbia)
Hudson Bay Divide
Triple Divide Peak (True)
Marias Pass
lowest point on Montana's Continental Divide

Chinese Wall

Triple Divide Peak (Bob Marshall)
Scapegoat Mountain

Rogers Pass
site of U.S. cold temperature record

Granite Butte RNA (proposed)

Thunderbolt Mtn. RNA (proposed)
Bernice RNA (proposed)
Dexter Basin RNA (proposed)
Cutaway Pass
highest Continental Divide pass
Goat Flat RNA (proposed)
East Fork Bitterroot RNA (proposed)

Basin Creek RNA (proposed)
Butte Water Co. interbasin transfer from Big Hole River
Point where Continental Divide leaves crest of Bitterroot Range
Cottonwood Peak
Eighteenmile Peak
highest point on Montana's Continental Divide
Italian Peak
southernmost point of Montana
Red Rock Lakes RNA

Cliff Lake RNA
Obsidian Sands RNA (proposed)
Intersection of Montana/Wyoming/Idaho on Continental Divide
Head of Hellroaring Creek, most distant source of Missouri

■ GEOGRAPHIC POINTS
■ PASSES
■ PEAKS
■ MOUNTAINS
■ RESEARCH NATURAL AREAS
■ POINTS OF INTEREST

Epilogue

As I write these final words I feel a strange mixture of relief, sadness and joy. Relief, certainly, that a demanding project is nearing completion. Sadness because I no longer have an excuse nor the time to return to the special places along the Divide that formed the backdrop for so much of this book. But mostly joy, as I reflect upon the hope that much of the Divide remains as the early explorers first saw it, and most of what I have seen will stay that way for the benefit of future generations.

Examples of preservation and exploitation are found along Montana's Continental Divide. But most of all, wise use prevails — the kind of stewardship based on the reality that there is no need to re-conquer the Great Barrier. In the fleeting span of little more than a century our agenda has changed from conquest to conservation.

Now when I think of the Continental Divide I think about the clouds, the unending wind, the fresh taste of rain, snow and ice during all seasons, the clarity of crisp high-altitude air and changing terrain that mere words cannot begin to portray. I recall being cold, hot, and wet, sometimes all in a single hour. I see dim figures in the trail ahead of me. Are they an Indian hunting party, Lewis and Clark, fur trappers, railroad surveyors?

Join with me, and let your imagination wander to its limits.

Sources

Alt, D., C. Buckholtz, B. Gildart, and B. Frauson. *Montana's Glacier National Park*. Helena, Mont.: Montana Magazine, Inc., 1983.

Alwin, J.A. *Western Montana: A Portrait of the Land and its People*. Helena, Mont.; Montana Magazine, Inc., 1983.

American West Editors. *The Magnificent Rockies*. Palo Alto, Calif.: American West Publishing Company, 1973.

Arno, S.F. *Forest Regions of Montana*. USDA Forest Service Research Paper INT-218. Ogden, Utah: Intermountain Forest & Range Experiment Station, USDA Forest Service, April 1979.

Arno, S.F. *Timberline*. Seattle, Wash.: The Mountaineers, 1984.

Borah, L.A. "Montana, Shining Mountain Treasureland." *National Geographic,* June 1950.

Burk, D. *Montana*. Portland, Ore.: Graphic Arts Center Publishing Co., 1980.

Chapman, R.H. "Our Northern Rockies." *National Geographic,* October 1902.

Cheney, R.C. *Names on the Face of Montana*. Missoula, Mont.: Univ. of Montana, 1971; Mountain Press Publishing Company, 1983.

Cordell, G. *Climate of Montana*. U.S. Department of Commerce Publication No. 60-24. Washington: U.S. Government Printing Office, 1971.

Craighead, J., and J. Mitchell. "The Grizzly Bear." Chapter 25 in *Wild Animals of North America*. Baltimore: Johns Hopkins University Press, 1982.

Cunningham, B. "The Anaconda-Pintlers." *Montana Magazine,* July-August 1984: 14-16.

Cunningham, B. "Bob Marshall Wilderness: East Side." *Montana Magazine,* September-October 1985: 79-86.

Cunningham, B. "Great Bear—Big River." *Montana Magazine,* July-August 1985: 76-80.

Cunningham, B. "Symphony at Red Rocks." *Montana Magazine,* March-April 1985: 50-52.

Cunningham, C., comp. *Montana Weather*. Helena, Mont.: Montana Magazine, Inc., 1982.

DeVoto, B., ed. *Journals of Lewis and Clark*. Boston: Houghton-Mifflin, 1953.

Dightman, R.A. *Climate of Glacier National Park, Montana*. Kalispell, Mont.: Glacier Natural History Association, National Park Service and U.S. Weather Bureau, Bulletin No. 7, May 1967.

Edwards, M. "Along the Great Divide." *National Geographic* October 1979: 483-515.

Gildart, R., with J. Wassink. *Montana Wildlife*. Helena, Mont.: Montana Magazine, Inc., 1982.

Seen from the top of the Chinese Wall, a shaft of late afternoon light hits Moose Creek. BILL CUNNINGHAM

Graetz, R. *Montana's Bob Marshall Country*. Helena, Mont.: Montana Magazine, Inc., 1985.

Guthrie, A.B., Jr. "The Great Rockies." *Holiday Magazine,* August 1963.

Knight, R. *The Sun River Elk Herd*. The Wildlife Society, Wildlife Monograph No. 23, October 1970.

Koch, E. "Big Game in Montana from Early Historical Records." *Journal of Wildlife Management* 5 (1941): 357-70.

Long, G.W. "Many-Splendored Glacierland." *National Geographic* May 1956: 589-630.

McClure, A.K. *Three Thousand Miles Through the Rocky Mountains*. Philadelphia: J.B. Lippincott & Company, 1869.

Mattson, U. "Search for Wolves." *Persimmon Hill* 13 (1983) 3:37-51.

Montana Wildlands Coalition. Information Sheets on the North Big Hole, West Big Hole, Lionhead, Electric Peak, Black Mountain, Nevada Mountain, and Italian Peaks roadless areas, 1984.

Payette, B.C. *The Mullan Road*. Montreal: Payette Radio Limited, 1968.

Picton, H.D. "Migration Patterns of the Sun River Elk Herd, Montana." *Journal of Wildlife Management* 24 (July 1960) 3:279-290.

Plassman, M.E., Unpublished reminiscences written during the 1920's and 1930's, Montana Historical Society Archives, Helena, Mont.

Reese, R. *Montana Mountain Ranges,* rev. ed. Helena, Mont.: Montana Magazine, Inc., 1985.

Renz, L. *History of the Northern Pacific Railroad*. Fairfield, Wash.: Ye Galleon Press, 1980.

Robbins, M. *Along the Continental Divide*. Washington, D.C.: National Geographic Society, 1981.

Ryhack, E. and T. *The Ultimate Journey: Canada to Mexico Down the Continental Divide*. San Francisco: Chronicle Books, 1973.

Shaw, C. *The Flathead Story*. Missoula, Mont.: U.S. Forest Service, July 1964.

Smalley, E.V. *History of the Northern Pacific Railroad*. New York: G.P. Putnam & Sons, 1883.

Sprague, M. *The Great Gates*. Lincoln: University of Nebraska Press, 1964.

"Sun Road Golden Anniversary." Columbia Falls, Mont.: *Hungry Horse News/Waterton-Glacier Times,* Special Edition, July 15, 1983.

Thompson, L.S. *Montana's Explorers: The Pioneer Naturalists*. Helena, Mont.: Montana Magazine, Inc., 1985.

Trenton, P., and P. Hassrick. *The Rocky Mountains: A Vision for Artists in the Nineteenth Century*. Norman: University of Oklahoma Press, 1983.

U.S. Forest Service. *Early Days in the Forest Service* Volume I. Missoula, Mont.: U.S. Forest Service, October 15, 1944.

U.S. Geological Survey. *Mineral and Water Resources of Montana*. Senate Document No. 98. Prepared at the request of Senator Lee Metcalf of Montana. Washington: U.S. Government Printing Office, 1968.

Walker, B.S. *The Great Divide*. New York: Time-Life Books, 1973.

Wolle, M. *Montana Pay Dirt: A Guide to the Mining Camps of the Treasure State*. Denver: Sage Books, 1963.

Wood, C.R. and D.M. *Milwaukee Road West*. Seattle, WA: Superior Publishing Company, 1972.

Woodruff, S., and D. Schwennesen. *Montana Wilderness: Discovering the Heritage*. Kansas City, Missouri: *The Missoulian* and Lowell Press, 1984.

Wolf, J.R. *Guide to the Continental Divide Trail: Volume I, Northern Montana*. Missoula, Mont.: Mountain Press Publishing Company, 1976.

Wolf, J.R. *Guide to the Continental Divide Trail: Southern Montana and Idaho*. Washington: Continental Divide Trail Society, 1979.

Next in the Montana Geographic Series

Eastern Montana Mountain Ranges

Sentinels of the plains, the isolated mountain ranges of Eastern Montana offer magnificent vistas not found in Western Montana. The so-called mountain outiers are unique as Montana mountain ranges to — well-defined bodies visible from tens of miles on the prairie landscape. This little-known resource includes the Snowy, Judith, Moccasin, Big and Little Belt, Highwood, Crazy, Bighorn, and Pryor ranges as well as other landmarks such as the Sweetgrass Hills and Square Butte of central and northcentral Montana and the Chalk Buttes and Medicine Rocks of southeastern Montana. You'll discover how these intrusions on the vast plain came to be and how they contribute to the local history and economy. You'll visit each and learn of its recreational opportunities. This volume makes an excellent companion to Mountain Ranges of Montana, first in the Geographic Series, which concentrated on Western Montana. By Mark Meloy.

Montana's Flathead River Country

Its North Fork comes from Glacier Park Country. Its Middle and South forks emanate from the heart of the Bob Marshall Wilderness. The lake that shares its name is a national magnet. It is the Flathead River system and its significance to Montana is profound. This book tells of its natural history — the wildlands, the waters, the wildlife; and its human history —how the Flathead Valley was settled, steamboats on the lake, the cherry industry. And you'll visit the beautiful Flathead country today — see communities as diverse as Polebridge, Bigfork and Kalispell, learn about recreation on the lake and the river, and follow the little known part of the river from Kerr Dam to the Clark's Fork River. By Bert Gildart, author of *Montana's Missouri River,* and co-author of *Glacier Country* and *Montana's Wildlife* — all books in the Montana Geographic Series.

The Montana Geographic Series:

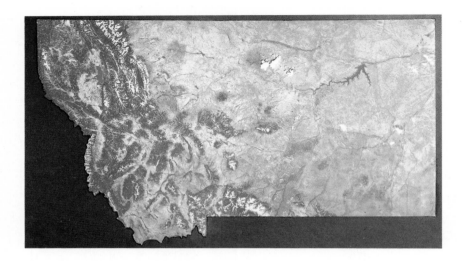

About Our Back Cover Photo
This photographic mosaic was compiled from Earth Resources Satellite Photo passes made from a height of 570 miles. It was pieced together in black and white and interpreted in color by Big Sky Magic, Larry Dodge, Owner.
Commercial Color Adaptation © 1976 Big Sky Magic.

Front cover photographs

Clockwise from upper right:

The Continental Divide north of Pyramid Peak. BILL CUNNINGHAM

Reynolds Mountain, Glacier National Park. JEFF GNASS

In the Bob Marshall Wilderness. BILL CUNNINGHAM

Atop Red Rock Pass. BILL CUNNINGHAM

Montana-Idaho boundary stake. CHARLES KAY

On Homestake Pass. GEORGE WUERTHNER